DAVID BEN-GURION

WORLD LEADERS — PAST & PRESENT

DAVID BEN-GURION

John J. Vail

CHELSEA HOUSE PUBLISHERS
NEW YORK
NEW HAVEN   PHILADELPHIA

EDITOR-IN-CHIEF: Nancy Toff
EXECUTIVE EDITOR: Remmel T. Nunn
MANAGING EDITOR: Karyn Gullen Browne
COPY CHIEF: Juliann Barbato
ART DIRECTOR: Giannella Garrett
MANUFACTURING MANAGER: Gerald Levine

Staff for DAVID BEN-GURION:

SENIOR EDITOR: John W. Selfridge
ASSISTANT EDITORS: Maria Behan, Pierre Hauser, Kathleen McDermott, Bert Yaeger
EDITORIAL ASSISTANT: James Guiry
COPY EDITORS: Gillian Bucky, Sean Dolan, Ellen Scordato
PICTURE EDITOR: Juliette Dickstein
DESIGN ASSISTANT: Jill Goldreyer
PICTURE RESEARCH: Cheryl Moch
LAYOUT: Ghila Krajzman
PRODUCTION COORDINATOR: Laura McCormick
COVER ILLUSTRATION: © Michael Garland

CREATIVE DIRECTOR: Harold Steinberg

Copyright © 1987 by Chelsea House Publishers, a division of Main Line Book Co. All rights reserved.
Printed and bound in the United States of America.

Frontispiece courtesy of David Ben-Gurion Centennial Commission

First Printing

Library of Congress Cataloging in Publication Data

Vail, John J. DAVID BEN-GURION.

(World leaders past & present)
Bibliography: p.
Includes index.
1. Ben-Gurion, David, 1886–1973. 2. Prime ministers—Israel—Biography. 3. Zionists—Palestine—Biography. I. Title. II. Series: World leaders past & present.
DS125.3.B37V35   1987   956.94′05′0924 [B] 87-9323

ISBN 0-87754-509-X

Contents

"On Leadership," Arthur M. Schlesinger, jr. 7
 1. Exiles' Return 13
 2. The Young Lion 25
 3. Labor Zionism 37
 4. The Age of Nazism 47
 5. The Division of Palestine 55
 6. The Soldier 63
 7. War of Independence 71
 8. Prime Minister 83
 9. A Famous Kibbutznik 91
10. And the Deserts Will Bloom 101
Further Reading 108
Chronology 109
Index 110

CHELSEA HOUSE PUBLISHERS
WORLD LEADERS PAST & PRESENT

ADENAUER
ALEXANDER THE GREAT
MARC ANTONY
KING ARTHUR
ATATÜRK
ATTLEE
BEGIN
BEN-GURION
BISMARCK
LÉON BLUM
BOLÍVAR
CESARE BORGIA
BRANDT
BREZHNEV
CAESAR
CALVIN
CASTRO
CATHERINE THE GREAT
CHARLEMAGNE
CHIANG KAI-SHEK
CHURCHILL
CLEMENCEAU
CLEOPATRA
CORTÉS
CROMWELL
DANTON
DE GAULLE
DE VALERA
DISRAELI
EISENHOWER
ELEANOR OF AQUITAINE
QUEEN ELIZABETH I
FERDINAND AND ISABELLA
FRANCO

FREDERICK THE GREAT
INDIRA GANDHI
MOHANDAS GANDHI
GARIBALDI
GENGHIS KHAN
GLADSTONE
GORBACHEV
HAMMARSKJÖLD
HENRY VIII
HENRY OF NAVARRE
HINDENBURG
HITLER
HO CHI MINH
HUSSEIN
IVAN THE TERRIBLE
ANDREW JACKSON
JEFFERSON
JOAN OF ARC
POPE JOHN XXIII
LYNDON JOHNSON
JUÁREZ
JOHN F. KENNEDY
KENYATTA
KHOMEINI
KHRUSHCHEV
MARTIN LUTHER KING, JR.
KISSINGER
LENIN
LINCOLN
LLOYD GEORGE
LOUIS XIV
LUTHER
JUDAS MACCABEUS
MAO ZEDONG

MARY, QUEEN OF SCOTS
GOLDA MEIR
METTERNICH
MUSSOLINI
NAPOLEON
NASSER
NEHRU
NERO
NICHOLAS II
NIXON
NKRUMAH
PERICLES
PERÓN
QADDAFI
ROBESPIERRE
ELEANOR ROOSEVELT
FRANKLIN D. ROOSEVELT
THEODORE ROOSEVELT
SADAT
STALIN
SUN YAT-SEN
TAMERLANE
THATCHER
TITO
TROTSKY
TRUDEAU
TRUMAN
VICTORIA
WASHINGTON
WEIZMANN
WOODROW WILSON
XERXES
ZHOU ENLAI

ON LEADERSHIP
Arthur M. Schlesinger, jr.

LEADERSHIP, it may be said, is really what makes the world go round. Love no doubt smooths the passage; but love is a private transaction between consenting adults. Leadership is a public transaction with history. The idea of leadership affirms the capacity of individuals to move, inspire, and mobilize masses of people so that they act together in pursuit of an end. Sometimes leadership serves good purposes, sometimes bad; but whether the end is benign or evil, great leaders are those men and women who leave their personal stamp on history.

Now, the very concept of leadership implies the proposition that individuals can make a difference. This proposition has never been universally accepted. From classical times to the present day, eminent thinkers have regarded individuals as no more than the agents and pawns of larger forces, whether the gods and goddesses of the ancient world or, in the modern era, race, class, nation, the dialectic, the will of the people, the spirit of the times, history itself. Against such forces, the individual dwindles into insignificance.

So contends the thesis of historical determinism. Tolstoy's great novel *War and Peace* offers a famous statement of the case. Why, Tolstoy asked, did millions of men in the Napoleonic wars, denying their human feelings and their common sense, move back and forth across Europe slaughtering their fellows? "The war," Tolstoy answered, "was bound to happen simply because it was bound to happen." All prior history predetermined it. As for leaders, they, Tolstoy said, "are but the labels that serve to give a name to an end and, like labels, they have the least possible connection with the event." The greater the leader, "the more conspicuous the inevitability and the predestination of every act he commits." The leader, said Tolstoy, is "the slave of history."

Determinism takes many forms. Marxism is the determinism of class. Nazism the determinism of race. But the idea of men and women as the slaves of history runs athwart the deepest human instincts. Rigid determinism abolishes the idea of human freedom—

the assumption of free choice that underlies every move we make, every word we speak, every thought we think. It abolishes the idea of human responsibility, since it is manifestly unfair to reward or punish people for actions that are by definition beyond their control. No one can live consistently by any deterministic creed. The Marxist states prove this themselves by their extreme susceptibility to the cult of leadership.

More than that, history refutes the idea that individuals make no difference. In December 1931 a British politician crossing Park Avenue in New York City between 76th and 77th Streets around 10:30 P.M. looked in the wrong direction and was knocked down by an automobile—a moment, he later recalled, of a man aghast, a world aglare: "I do not understand why I was not broken like an eggshell or squashed like a gooseberry." Fourteen months later an American politician, sitting in an open car in Miami, Florida, was fired on by an assassin; the man beside him was hit. Those who believe that individuals make no difference to history might well ponder whether the next two decades would have been the same had Mario Constasino's car killed Winston Churchill in 1931 and Giuseppe Zangara's bullet killed Franklin Roosevelt in 1933. Suppose, in addition, that Adolf Hitler had been killed in the street fighting during the Munich *Putsch* of 1923 and that Lenin had died of typhus during World War I. What would the 20th century be like now?

For better or for worse, individuals do make a difference. "The notion that a people can run itself and its affairs anonymously," wrote the philosopher William James, "is now well known to be the silliest of absurdities. Mankind does nothing save through initiatives on the part of inventors, great or small, and imitation by the rest of us—these are the sole factors in human progress. Individuals of genius show the way, and set the patterns, which common people then adopt and follow."

Leadership, James suggests, means leadership in thought as well as in action. In the long run, leaders in thought may well make the greater difference to the world. But, as Woodrow Wilson once said, "Those only are leaders of men, in the general eye, who lead in action. . . . It is at their hands that new thought gets its translation into the crude language of deeds." Leaders in thought often invent in solitude and obscurity, leaving to later generations the tasks of imitation. Leaders in action—the leaders portrayed in this series—have to be effective in their own time.

And they cannot be effective by themselves. They must act in response to the rhythms of their age. Their genius must be adapted, in a phrase of William James's, "to the receptivities of the moment." Leaders are useless without followers. "There goes the mob," said the French politician hearing a clamor in the streets. "I am their leader. I must follow them." Great leaders turn the inchoate emotions of the mob to purposes of their own. They seize on the opportunities of their time, the hopes, fears, frustrations, crises, potentialities. They succeed when events have prepared the way for them, when the community is awaiting to be aroused, when they can provide the clarifying and organizing ideas. Leadership ignites the circuit between the individual and the mass and thereby alters history.

It may alter history for better or for worse. Leaders have been responsible for the most extravagant follies and most monstrous crimes that have beset suffering humanity. They have also been vital in such gains as humanity has made in individual freedom, religious and racial tolerance, social justice and respect for human rights.

There is no sure way to tell in advance who is going to lead for good and who for evil. But a glance at the gallery of men and women in *World Leaders—Past and Present* suggests some useful tests.

One test is this: do leaders lead by force or by persuasion? By command or by consent? Through most of history leadership was exercised by the divine right of authority. The duty of followers was to defer and to obey. "Theirs not to reason why,/ Theirs but to do and die." On occasion, as with the so-called "enlightened despots" of the 18th century in Europe, absolutist leadership was animated by humane purposes. More often, absolutism nourished the passion for domination, land, gold and conquest and resulted in tyranny.

The great revolution of modern times has been the revolution of equality. The idea that all people should be equal in their legal condition has undermined the old structure of authority, hierarchy and deference. The revolution of equality has had two contrary effects on the nature of leadership. For equality, as Alexis de Tocqueville pointed out in his great study *Democracy in America,* might mean equality in servitude as well as equality in freedom.

"I know of only two methods of establishing equality in the political world," Tocqueville wrote. "Rights must be given to every citizen, or none at all to anyone . . . save one, who is the master of all." There was no middle ground "between the sovereignty of all and the absolute power of one man." In his astonishing prediction of 20th-century totalitarian dictatorship, Tocqueville explained how the revolution of equality could lead to the *"Führerprinzip"* and more terrible absolutism than the world had ever known.

But when rights are given to every citizen and the sovereignty of all is established, the problem of leadership takes a new form, becomes more exacting than ever before. It is easy to issue commands and enforce them by the rope and the stake, the concentration camp and the *gulag*. It is much harder to use argument and achievement to overcome opposition and win consent. The Founding Fathers of the United States understood the difficulty. They believed that history had given them the opportunity to decide, as Alexander Hamilton wrote in the first Federalist Paper, whether men are indeed capable of basing government on "reflection and choice, or whether they are forever destined to depend . . . on accident and force."

Government by reflection and choice called for a new style of leadership and a new quality of followership. It required leaders to be responsive to popular concerns, and it required followers to be active and informed participants in the process. Democracy does not eliminate emotion from politics; sometimes it fosters demagoguery; but it is confident that, as the greatest of democratic leaders put it, you cannot fool all of the people all of the time. It measures leadership by results and retires those who overreach or falter or fail.

It is true that in the long run despots are measured by results too. But they can postpone the day of judgment, sometimes indefinitely, and in the meantime they can do infinite harm. It is also true that democracy is no guarantee of virtue and intelligence in government, for the voice of the people is not necessarily the voice of God. But democracy, by assuring the right of opposition, offers built-in resistance to the evils inherent in absolutism. As the theologian Reinhold Niebuhr summed it up, "Man's capacity for justice makes democracy possible, but man's inclination to injustice makes democracy necessary."

A second test for leadership is the end for which power is sought. When leaders have as their goal the supremacy of a master race or the promotion of totalitarian revolution or the acquisition and exploitation of colonies or the protection of greed and privilege or the preservation of personal power, it is likely that their leadership will do little to advance the cause of humanity. When their goal is the abolition of slavery, the liberation of women, the enlargement of opportunity for the poor and powerless, the extension of equal rights to racial minorities, the defense of the freedoms of expression and opposition, it is likely that their leadership will increase the sum of human liberty and welfare.

Leaders have done great harm to the world. They have also conferred great benefits. You will find both sorts in this series. Even "good" leaders must be regarded with a certain wariness. Leaders are not demigods; they put on their trousers one leg after another just like ordinary mortals. No leader is infallible, and every leader needs to be reminded of this at regular intervals. Irreverence irritates leaders but is their salvation. Unquestioning submission corrupts leaders and demands followers. Making a cult of a leader is always a mistake. Fortunately hero worship generates its own antidote. "Every hero," said Emerson, "becomes a bore at last."

The signal benefit the great leaders confer is to embolden the rest of us to live according to our own best selves, to be active, insistent, and resolute in affirming our own sense of things. For great leaders attest to the reality of human freedom against the supposed inevitabilities of history. And they attest to the wisdom and power that may lie within the most unlikely of us, which is why Abraham Lincoln remains the supreme example of great leadership. A great leader, said Emerson, exhibits new possibilities to all humanity. "We feed on genius. . . . Great men exist that there may be greater men."

Great leaders, in short, justify themselves by emancipating and empowering their followers. So humanity struggles to master its destiny, remembering with Alexis de Tocqueville: "It is true that around every man a fatal circle is traced beyond which he cannot pass; but within the wide verge of that circle he is powerful and free; as it is with man, so with communities."

1
Exiles' Return

Just before 4 P.M. on May 14, 1948, a black limousine pulled up to a small museum in Tel Aviv. A crowd of onlookers applauded vigorously and waved aloft blue and white flags emblazoned with the Star of David (the ancestral symbol of the Jewish people) as a short, stocky man with a halo of white hair stepped out of the car. Pausing briefly, the man waved to the cheering crowd, then climbed the stairs and disappeared into the building. The man was David Ben-Gurion. Today he would fulfill a dream that had driven him since his youth. Today, as head of the National Council, the body governing Jews living in Palestine, he would lead a ceremony establishing the Jewish state of Israel. Today, the Jews, after 2,000 years of exile from their ancestral land, years during which they had been driven from country to country, years of persecution and poverty, would again have a home.

> *In Israel, in order to be a realist, you must believe in miracles.*
> —DAVID BEN-GURION

David Ben-Gurion and his wife, Paula, arrive on May 14, 1948, at the Tel Aviv Museum, where he would preside over a ceremony officially establishing the independent Jewish state of Israel. Ben-Gurion became the head of the new nation's provisional government.

AP/WIDE WORLD

Flanked by other members of the National Council and standing beneath a portrait of Theodor Herzl, the founder of Zionism, Ben-Gurion reads the historic Proclamation of Independence of the State of Israel.

Inside the Tel Aviv Museum, Ben-Gurion joined a group of 12 men sitting behind a long wooden table. Dominating the hall was a portrait of Dr. Theodor Herzl, the 19th-century Austrian playwright who had transformed the vague yearnings of European Jews for a homeland into a modern political movement known as Zionism. On the other walls were paintings by Jewish artists, including Marc Chagall's haunting masterpiece, "Jew Holding the Tablets." Ben-Gurion silently surveyed the spectators, who sat on brown, wooden chairs or stood in the crowded aisles. He recognized most of the faces. Many of them he had known since his first days in Palestine in the early 1900s, when the Jewish population there consisted of only a few communal farms struggling to wring life out of the inhospitable desert. Others had joined him later in lobbying foreign governments to lend support to the idea of a homeland. Scattered about the museum were reporters and press photographers who had come from around the world to capture this historic moment.

At precisely 4 P.M., Ben-Gurion rose in front of the gathering. Though since his days as a farming pioneer in Palestine he had usually dressed informally, today he wore a dark suit and a tie. After he struck a gavel on the table, the spectators spontaneously rose to their feet and sang a traditional Jewish song called "Hatikvah," a Hebrew word that means "the hope." (Hebrew is the biblical language of the Jews, and it also became the language of the state of Israel.) The "Hatikvah" had never been performed with such pride. It would eventually become the anthem of the new nation. After it was finished, Ben-Gurion began to read the Proclamation of Independence of the State of Israel: "The Land of Israel was the birthplace of the Jewish people. Here their spiritual, religious, and national identity was formed. Here they achieved independence and created a culture of national and universal significance. Here they wrote and gave the Bible to the world. Exiled from the Land of Israel, the Jewish people remained faithful to it in all the centuries of their dispersion, never ceasing to pray and hope for their return and the restoration of their national freedom." Ben-Gurion's words resounded throughout the quiet gallery; people were motionless, transfixed, afraid that a single cough or movement would somehow detract from the solemn dignity of the occasion.

Ben-Gurion reached the end of the Proclamation: "We hereby proclaim the establishment of the Jewish state in Palestine, to be called the State of Israel." With this proclamation the entire crowd rose to its feet and burst into an emotional encore of "Hatikvah." People tearfully embraced and congratulated each other. Outside the hall the streets of Tel Aviv were alive with joyous celebrations.

Only 37 minutes were needed to proclaim the independence of a people who had struggled for their freedom for almost 2,000 years. But as Ben-Gurion walked triumphantly from the hall, his face betrayed his ambivalence; he told his wife, "I feel like a

We are a people — one people. We are strong enough to form a state and indeed a model state.
—THEODOR HERZL
In *The Jewish State*

A turn-of-the-century view of Plonsk, a typical Russian *shtetl* (market town), shows Jewish residents gathering water at a communal well. David Green was born in Plonsk in 1886.

mourner at the feast." Ben-Gurion realized that at the stroke of midnight, the state of Israel, barely eight hours old, would be faced with an all-out war for survival. Ben-Gurion's historic journey had truly just begun.

Ben-Gurion first dreamed of establishing a homeland for the Jews during his childhood in Poland, which was then a territory in the Russian empire. Russia kept its Jewish population confined to an area called the pale of settlement — the eastern portion of Poland, Belorussia, Lithuania, and the northeastern Ukraine. Inside the pale, most Jews lived in *shtetls*, small market towns to which they had retreated after being driven from rural areas by Russian tsar Nicholas II during the 1850s. In addition to residential restrictions, Jews in Russian Poland had to endure severe economic hardship and frequent periods of anti-Semitic violence. Admissions quotas kept most Jews from obtaining secondary and higher education outside their own schools. They were barred from several vocations, including law, medicine, the civil services, academia, and heavy industry. Those who managed to secure positions in light industry were subjected to the horrendous working conditions typical in the early part of the Industrial Revolution.

With few options available to them, the majority of Jewish men became self-supporting tradesmen engaged primarily in the garment industry in which fierce competition kept prices and profit margins low. Thirty to thirty-five percent of the Jewish population relied on relief from Jewish welfare organizations. Jews also were made the target of an extensive propaganda effort by the Russian government to identify them with everything "western" during a period of intense Russian chauvinism. Throughout the empire, posters warned of the Jewish menace under the headline *"Zhid idyot"* ("The Jew is upon you").

Residential restrictions and persecution encouraged Polish Jews in their tendency to remain apart from the surrounding society, to shun assimilation. They had their own style of dress, they spoke their own language, they attended their own schools, they married only other Jews, and above all they followed their own religion.

Ben-Gurion was born David Green, the sixth child of Avigdor and Sheindel Green, in a Polish shtetl called Plonsk on October 16, 1886. His early years were unusual for a Jewish child in Poland in that he had very little direct experience of anti-Semitism and economic deprivation. Though residents of Plonsk were subject to all of Russia's anti-Jewish laws, the town managed to escape most of the brutal campaigns of anti-Semitic violence, or *pogroms*, that swept the rest of Poland during the period. And though most of the town's residents were poor, the Greens lived quite comfortably.

The family owned two handsomely decorated two-story houses at the end of a relatively uncongested roadway called Goat's Street. While renting out one house, the family occupied the first level of the other, giving up the second floor to a family of servants who cooked meals, cleaned the house, and tended the animals that grazed in the garden. David's father, Avigdor, a well-educated and vivacious man, was employed as a "Jewish advocate," an official responsible for writing petitions in favor of Jewish causes and for legal counseling to Jews — though he was prohibited by Russian law from actually appearing in court. His work won him prominence in the Jewish community and brought him in contact with the Polish population and the Russian authorities. He was handsome, tall, and was known for being the first Jew in town to discard traditional Jewish clothing — a long caftan and a fur hat — for a black suitcoat, large bow tie, striped trousers, and a silk hat. He even smoked cigarettes, an unforgivable sin among more orthodox Jews.

Though Avigdor ignored many of the strictures of the Jewish religion, he remained devoted to the Jewish nation. He participated in the lively Jewish intellectual life of Plonsk as a member of the Society of Friends of Learning, a volunteer group dedicated to spreading interest in the Bible and Hebrew grammar to the lower classes. His father, David's grandfather, Zvi Aryeh Green, was one of the founders of the society. A man who influenced David a great deal, Zvi Green was a former professor and a devoutly religious man who read at least five books of the Bible every day. In addition to speaking Polish and Yiddish (the everyday language of Russian and Polish Jews), he was also fluent in Russian, German, and Hebrew.

Members of the Green clan were also passionately committed to Zionism, a movement gradually gaining force across Europe that had as its objective the re-creation of a Jewish state in Palestine. In the second half of the 19th century, a number of Zionist groups had sprung up independently of one another in several European countries. In France, the movement was spearheaded by historian Joseph Salvador and Baron Edmond de Rothschild, in Germany by Rabbi Hirsch Kalisher and the socialist Moses Hess, and in Britain by Moses Montefiore and Lawrence Oliphant. The idea of Jewish statehood also was celebrated by several writers of the time, including George Eliot in her novel *Daniel Deronda*.

In Russia, a brutal wave of pogroms that followed the assassination of Tsar Alexander II made Zion-

The goal of Zionism, a political movement that developed in Europe during the late 19th century, was the re-establishment of a Jewish homeland in Palestine. Theodor Herzl, the movement's founder, assembled the first Zionist Congress in 1897.

ism particularly popular. The Russian Zionist organization, called *Hovevei Zion* (Lovers of Zion), was founded in 1882 by Leon Pinsker, who set forth his group's guiding principles in his seminal book, *Auto-Emancipation*. Pinsker argued that, as minority groups in foreign nations ruled by others, Jews would always be subject to persecution — because, to his mind, anti-Semitism was an incurable psychological disease. Pinsker was a political Zionist — one who favored the creation of a Jewish state in order to guarantee the rights of the Jews as a national group, but not necessarily in order to perpetuate the religion of Judaism. Other Zionists, called religious Zionists, sought a Jewish homeland that would be primarily a religious community governed by the Torah, sacred laws contained in Jewish scripture. Religious Zionists considered the Jews to be entitled to a state in Palestine because according to the Bible they were God's chosen people, while political Zionists considered the Jews deserving of a state simply because they were a nation of people. As a follower of Pinsker and a member of Lovers of Zion, Avigdor Green was himself a political Zionist.

In 1884 he became one of the leading missionaries of the Lovers of Zion. He lectured at conferences across Russia, and the Greens' house on Goat's Street became the headquarters of the local chapter. Meetings were convened at all hours of the day and night, and a constant parade of friends, visitors, and advice seekers gathered at the house. David Green grew up in this heady atmosphere of intellectual freedom and lively political debate. From an early age, he was taught by his father about Zionism. Listening to his father's bedtime tales about early Jewish heroes, the young boy often fell asleep dreaming of the ancient Jewish homeland. He later wrote, "It is no exaggeration to say that at three I had dreams of coming to Palestine. And certainly from my tenth year on, I never thought of spending my life anywhere else." Part of the plan for reestablishing a Jewish state in Palestine was to revive the biblical forefathers' language. Thus, David Green began at the age of three to learn Hebrew while sitting on his grandfather's knee.

DAVID BEN-GURION CENTENNIAL COMMISSION

David Green resolved at an early age to dedicate his life to the creation of a Jewish state in Palestine. At age 18 he joined *Poalei Zion* (Workers of Zion), a Polish political party that combined Zionism with socialist ideology.

If you will it, it is no dream.
—THEODOR HERZL

David was a serious, introspective child. He had few friends his own age and seldom took part in normal boyhood activities. While other children romped in the streets, David practiced his Hebrew lessons and played chess with his siblings and his father. He excelled at chess and learned to value tactics and strategy. At the age of eight, by which time he had mastered Hebrew, he began attending a school for gifted children. Everyone quickly recognized that David was the most brilliant child in class. One afternoon, his teacher was astounded as David, after listening to a classmate read a page from the Bible, repeated the passage back word-for-word.

Young David had a special relationship with his mother. Sheindel Green was a warm, loving, charitable woman. Because David was sickly and frail, every summer his mother took him to visit relatives in the countryside where he could rest and breathe fresh air. Sheindel continually built up her son's self-confidence; despite his poor health, the young boy had a quick, lively intelligence and his mother was absolutely convinced that he was destined for greatness. An inner strength that resulted from his mother's faith in him became an integral feature of David's character. One friend later remarked that Ben-Gurion "unconsciously believed he was blessed with a spark from Joshua's soul. This helped give him the will to succeed, a sense of destiny."

When David was 11 years old, his world suddenly collapsed. His mother, only 41, died in childbirth. For months afterward, David could not eat or sleep and lost interest in everything. "I used to see her in my dreams, regularly for almost two years," David said many years later. "Night after night, almost, I would dream about her, speak to her and ask her why she did not come back." Because his brothers and sisters were older and his father was always busy with work and political activities, David had no one to confide in. Ultimately, he overcame the tragedy by relying on his own inner strength. He emerged from it a much more mature youth than he had been before.

> *We have a son who will one day be known the world over.*
> —SHEINDEL GREEN
> Ben-Gurion's mother

That same year, Theodor Herzl emerged as the preeminent leader of Zionism. Earlier in his career, he had urged Jews to assimilate into European society in order to escape repression. But in 1894 he had been converted to the Zionist viewpoint after watching an appalling wave of anti-Semitism sweep Europe in response to the Dreyfus affair in France. Alfred Dreyfus, a Jewish captain in the French army, had been wrongly convicted of selling valuable military secrets to Germany, and after the trial anti-Semitic journals had pointed to the case as evidence of a Jewish plot to undermine the governments of Europe. Outraged by these developments, Herzl published a pamphlet in 1896 called *Der Judenstaat* (*The Jewish State*), which quickly became one of the key texts of the Zionist movement. He argued in his essay that Jews would not be accepted as equals by the rest of the world until they established their own nation. Such a nation, Herzl proposed, would preferably, but not necessarily, be located in Palestine and would be established through international diplomacy. In 1897 Herzl organized a Zionist conference in Basel, Switzerland. At the meeting, he forged the disparate factions of the European movement into an international network called the World Zionist Organization. The organization was to promote Zionism by raising funds for immigration and the purchase of land in Palestine and by encouraging through diplomacy other nations to support a Jewish state.

At the age of 14, David Green joined several friends in founding *Ezra*, a youth club that encouraged the study of Hebrew among the residents of Plonsk and promoted emigration to Palestine. In 1903 Ezra members raised funds to help the victims of the Kisinev pogrom, a recent attack on Jews in another region of the pale. That same year, Green and his friends were dismayed to hear that Herzl had proposed the establishment of a Jewish state in the highlands of Kenya, under British protection. For David, Zionism represented a spiritual need of the Jewish people that could be realized only by establishing a nation in the historic land of Israel.

THE BETTMANN ARCHIVE

The cover of a French newspaper shows Alfred Dreyfus, a Jewish captain in the French army, suffering public humiliation after his 1894 conviction on false charges of selling military secrets to Germany.

He and his friends decided the time had come to act. They had listened to too much empty talk, sat through too many meetings and speeches. The time had come to emigrate to Palestine. Because between them they only had sufficient funds to pay for one voyage, the three drew lots to determine who would be the first to leave. His friend Shlomo Zemach won. Until he had enough money to emigrate himself, Green decided to go to Warsaw to acquire an engineering degree; skilled pioneers would be extremely valuable in the new land.

After eight months David still had not left for Warsaw, for he was madly in love. David had met Rachel Nelkin when he was only 12 but had been at first too shy to express his feelings for her. Though he had secretly written love poems to her, he never dared send them. When he finally summoned the courage to confess his love, he was shocked to learn that it was reciprocated. Rachel also shared David's dream of traveling to the Holy Land. But since she was reluctant to leave for Palestine until her family could depart with her, David repeatedly postponed his plans.

But he gradually became ashamed that he had let his emotions interfere with his devotion to Zionism. Eventually, he decided to go to Warsaw, in spite of his attachment to Rachel, as a way of testing his character, of seeing whether he could overcome his sentimentality. Once there, he further challenged his resources, refusing to accept money from his

Green (front row, center, wearing a white shirt) and his girl friend Rachel Nelkin (to his right) pose with friends on the eve of their departure for Palestine in 1906. Green's decision to emigrate reflected his conviction that a Jewish state could be created only by Jews settling on the land, not merely by making speeches or organizing rallies.

Returning briefly from Palestine to Plonsk in 1910, Green poses with his siblings. As an introspective and serious child with few friends his own age, Green drew enormous strength from his family, spending much of his time playing chess with his brothers and sisters and learning Hebrew from his grandfather.

father, living in wretched quarters. It turned out that he could not attend a technical college because of quotas regulating Jewish admission to Russian universities. But he did become an active member of an organization called *Poalei Zion* (Workers of Zion), a group of Zionists who called for any future Jewish state to be established according to the blueprint of Karl Marx. David worked for Poalei Zion as a labor organizer. Returning temporarily to Plonsk, he organized the most exploited workers in town — seamstresses — into a union and led them in a prolonged walkout. Ultimately, the owners gave in to the inspired women, reducing the normal workday from 18 hours to 12 hours and promising increased wages. This was an important lesson for the future; in time David Green would attempt to harness the power of labor to build the new society in Palestine.

Shlomo Zemach had traveled to Palestine in November 1904 and since then had written David many detailed letters vividly describing his life there. David now felt he knew Palestine as well as the land of his birth. When Zemach returned for a brief visit to Plonsk in the summer of 1906, David finally decided it was time to leave for the Holy Land. He broke the news to his father and persuaded Rachel to come with him. In late summer, David, Shlomo Zemach, Rachel, and her mother boarded a Russian tanker for the long voyage. David was euphoric: it was unquestionably the happiest day in the young man's life. He was on his way to the land of his dreams with the woman he loved.

> *From my tenth year on, I never thought of spending my life anywhere else.*
> —DAVID BEN-GURION
> on his lifelong desire to live in Israel

2
The Young Lion

In the first morning light of September 1906, an aging Russian tanker neared the shore of Palestine. David Green, his heart pounding wildly, stood on deck and gazed through the mists of dawn at the outline of the coast. Minutes later, he walked down the gangplank to begin his new life in Palestine. The docks of Jaffa were a whirlwind of activity: porters rushed back and forth talking a babble of languages; vendors selling their homemade food and beverages descended upon the passengers. As he made his way through the city streets, Green was overwhelmed by the noise and squalor, the crowded alleyways, filthy bazaars, and hordes of beggars. Local Zionist organizations had arranged lodgings for Green in Jaffa but he was anxious to move on. "I could not resist an overpowering urge to see a Jewish village," he wrote years later.

So the same day that they arrived in Palestine, Green, Shlomo Zemach, and Rachel Nelkin set out on foot for Petach Tikvah (the "Gate of Hope" in English), one of about 20 Jewish agricultural settlements in Turkish-ruled Palestine. They traveled through fragrant orange groves, passed tall cypress trees waving in the wind, up steep hills offering panoramic views of the countryside. When Green

> *Whether I am a land-worker or a lawyer, I have only one aim: to work for the Jewish worker in Israel.*
> —DAVID GREEN
> on choosing an occupation, 1910

A view of the Old City of Jerusalem in 1900. On September 7, 1906, Green arrived in Palestine, which was then inhabited primarily by Arabs and ruled by the Ottoman Empire. It was a forgotten region of barren desert and corrupt, decaying cities.

THE BETTMANN ARCHIVE

THE BETTMANN ARCHIVE

Baron Edmond de Rothschild, a French banker and Zionist leader. During the 1880s, Rothschild gave substantial financial assistance to members of the first wave of Jewish immigration to Palestine. He bought land, established agricultural settlements, and sent advisers to aid the pioneers.

and his friends finally reached Petach Tikvah, the moonlit sky was ablaze with brilliant stars as far as the eye could see. This night would be forever engraved in Green's memory: "I lay awake — for who could sleep through this first night in the Land. The spirit of my childhood and my dreams had triumphed and I was joyous."

Unfortunately, Green found that by the harsh light of day Palestine was not quite the paradise his father had so lavishly portrayed in his bedtime stories. Centuries of war and neglect had left their mark on the country. The ancient land was dotted with large swamps infested with malarial flies, many old towns lay in ruins, and the soil had been eroded by years of misuse. Worst of all, many of the pioneers who had come during the first wave of immigration, known as the first *aliyah* (1882–84), had abandoned their original Zionist goals. Idealistic dreamers at the outset, many had become profit-minded landowners, who no longer worked their own land but instead depended on cheap Arab labor. Most of the farms had difficulty becoming economically self-sufficient and had to draw upon the support of Baron Edmond de Rothschild. The scion of a family of French-Jewish financiers, Rothschild poured money into construction, livestock, and land purchases.

On his second day in Palestine, Green obtained work as a day laborer in the orange groves hauling manure, planting trees, and picking fruit. "It is not easy work," he wrote his father, "and it calls for great patience and devotion for those who have never worked before . . . to withstand the summer heat and hoe the red clay. The sweat pours down, our hands are covered with calluses and sores and our limbs seem about to fall apart." Like many Jewish settlers, Green was stricken by malaria; his doctor warned that he would not survive the disease unless he left Palestine, but Green continued the back-breaking work in the fields.

Like many other members of the second aliyah (1904–1916), Green held idealistic notions about the value of this agricultural work. To him and the other young pioneers, farming was a way for the Jews to reestablish a connection to the land, which they considered an essential first step in building a new nation. Agricultural pioneering was also in keeping with the spirit of the Bible, which foresaw a "flowering of the deserts" upon the return of the Jews to Israel. On a more practical level, tilling the land would enable Jewish communities in Palestine to become economically self-sufficient and thus avoid dependence on the sometimes hostile surrounding society. Finally, on an emotional level, the visceral nature of farmwork gave Jews a tangible sense that they were advancing toward their goal.

To these young adventurers work took on an almost transcendental meaning. They constantly reminded each other that, in Hebrew, labor and worship are denoted by the same word, *avodah*. They proudly led ascetic lives, residing in sparse homes, wearing simple clothing, despising luxuries of any kind. A half-century later, the newly formed state of Israel would be led by the gray-haired survivors of these early farming days.

In 1907, one year after arriving in Palestine, Green moved to the Jewish settlement at Sejera in Galilee. Galilee was isolated frontier country. At Se-

Arriving in Palestine as part of the second wave of Jewish immigrants, Green initially found work as a poorly paid day farm laborer. He is pictured here in 1907 (center, barefoot) at Rishon le-Zion settlement, where for several months he stomped grapes in the wine cellars.

A farm established by members of the second *aliyah*. A year after arriving in Palestine, Green joined an agricultural collective in Galilee staffed entirely by other young, idealistic Jews.

jera there was no division between laborers and owners. While men planted and ploughed the fields, women tended the gardens and milked the cows. Here was everything young Green had imagined: "You feel yourself a partner in the act of creation." The settlement contained a mix of people from exotic lands: Jews from Kurdistan, Yemen (an Arab country in the Middle East), Russia, and Poland all linked together in a warm, communal atmosphere.

For Green, journeying to Galilee was, as Israeli historian Michael Bar-Zohar has written, "a Zionist act of profound significance." Galilee, the northern portion of Palestine between the Mediterranean Sea and the Jordan River, had been the last stronghold of the Jews after their expulsion from Jerusalem in 70 A.D. But Green's move to Sejera was prompted as much by personal reasons as by idealism. Green's relationship with Rachel Nelkin had deteriorated during his first year in Palestine. Rachel had been dismissed from her first job in the orange groves and had been unable to find a position at another settlement. Many of her partners were furious with her because her failure tarnished their own reputations as hard workers. In this time of duress, Rachel naturally looked to Green for support, but he was equally critical. Politics and personal life, for Green, were separate realms; his love for Rachel was still deep, but, as a Zionist committed to establishing a Jewish presence in Israel, he was disappointed by her poor performance. When Rachel hinted that she wanted to get married, Green ignored her, instead plunging even more furiously into his own work.

Feeling betrayed, Rachel began to spend time with Yehezkel Bet-Halachmi, a reserved young man who quickly fell in love with her. He was everything that Green was not: considerate, supportive, and willing to devote his time to her. Rachel's affair with Bet-Halachmi eventually destroyed her relationship with Green. It was at this time that he left for Galilee. A year after his departure, Rachel married Bet-Halachmi. Green continued to be deeply in love with Rachel, and it would be a long time before the ache in his heart disappeared.

For the most part, however, Green's stay in Galilee was one of the happiest times in his life. Sejera was the forerunner of the modern day *kibbutz*, a collective society where people shared in both the work and the profits and where everyone was united in a common bond of friendship and dependence. Green loved the cooperative atmosphere: he wrote to his father, "There is time to think and dream — and how would it be possible not to think when you strike along, plowing up the soil of the land of Israel, and all about you see Jews plowing the soil in their land." Green's fellow workers actually complained that his daydreaming, his planning for the future, distracted him from his labor. He often walked the farm's oxen while scanning the newspaper for news that might affect the future of Zionism. On one occasion, he looked up from reading and realized he was all alone in the field, with no oxen in sight. They had wandered off to another pasture. Such incidents convinced his peers that he would not remain a simple farmer, that he was destined for greater things.

The pioneers were soon given a glimpse of this future greatness. To protect Sejera from hostile Arabs in local villages and dangerous bandits who roamed the countryside, the Sejera farm foreman employed Circassian Arabs as watchmen. But many of the Jewish workers, including Green, did not like

> *It meant changing their personalities, discarding the accepted city-existence with its discreet entry into a comfortable niche.... They would go back to the land — The Land — and inherit a new majesty in the equality of labor.*
> —BARNET LITVINOFF
> British historian, on the second aliyah

Green and his close friend Yitzhak Ben-Zvi — the future president of Israel. At Ben-Zvi's invitation Green moved to Jerusalem in 1910 to serve on the editorial board of *Achdut* (*Unity*), the newspaper of Poalei Zion. At that time, Green changed his last name to Ben-Gurion to give his newspaper byline a biblical resonance.

having to depend on Arabs for their protection. Eventually, this group asked the farm foreman, who hired the Circassians, to leave the watchmen's job to residents of the settlement. The foreman refused to do so. Green knew that if he could expose the watchmen's negligence he might change the foreman's mind. Having spied on the Circassian watchmen for several nights, Green had discovered that they paid little attention to their jobs, depending on their past reputations as notorious thieves and hoodlums to keep trespassers out. Instead of patrolling the farm at night, they visited the neighboring villages and spent their time drinking with their friends.

Green planned an elaborate ruse. One night, when the watchman on duty was away from his post, Green led the foreman's finest mule out of the farm and placed it in hiding. He then informed the foreman that his prized animal had been stolen. When the foreman ran into the stables and found that the mule had disappeared, he shouted frantically for the watchman. But he was nowhere in the settlement. Messengers were sent into an Arab village where they found the watchman lying fast asleep. The foreman fired the Circassian and gave the job to one of the Jewish farmers. Soon every Jewish settlement had an armed Jewish watchman.

In time these watchmen became a united defense organization called *Hashomer*, the first Jewish defense organization of modern times. Helping to create Hashomer was Green's first significant contribution to the history of Israel.

In 1910 David Green, then 24 years old, moved to Jerusalem to join his friends Yitzhak Ben-Zvi and Rachel Yanait on the editorial board of *Achdut*, the official journal of Poalei Zion. He had decided that, because of his strong intellectual background, he could make a greater contribution to the Zionist cause by writing than by working in the fields. Other young writers on the paper had taken new names with biblical significance to dramatize their deep feeling for their homeland and their affinity for their ancestors. David Green followed suit, signing his first article under the last name Ben-Gurion, which in Hebrew meant "young lion." He later said that he chose the name "because it sounded like a name out of the Bible." From then on he would be known as David Ben-Gurion.

Ben-Gurion developed strong friendships with his fellow workers on the paper. He, Ben-Zvi, and Yanait became a familiar sight in the outdoor cafés of Jerusalem, where they would go to sip Turkish coffee and to discuss politics after long days of work. After these discussions, Ben-Gurion could often be found walking the streets alone, composing new articles and speeches in his head.

In 1912 Ben-Gurion left Palestine to study law in Constantinople, the capital of the Ottoman Empire. He had realized that the Jewish settlers had very little contact with their Turkish rulers and took small advantage of available legal channels in the empire to advance their interests. He hoped, as a lawyer in the Turkish courts, to rectify this situation. But before his legal career could get off the ground, World War I began. Turkey fought with Austria-Hungary and Germany against the Allied Powers. Not sure what role Palestinian Jews would play in the conflict, the Turks suspended their rights. Both Ben-Gurion and Ben-Zvi were expelled from the Ottoman Empire for conspiring to form a Jewish state.

> *Settlement of the land is the only Zionism I know. All the rest is a waste of time.*
> —DAVID GREEN
> 1908

Golda Meir picks tomatoes in Palestine in 1921. Born in Kiev, Russia, Meir, at age eight, moved with her family to Milwaukee, Wisconsin. There, during World War I, she met Ben-Gurion.

In May 1915 Ben-Gurion stood on the deck of yet another ship and this time gazed upon the silhouette of New York City's skyscrapers and the Statue of Liberty. With characteristic diligence and dedication, he had studied English during his month-long journey from Palestine to the United States. Ben-Gurion and Ben-Zvi were given a heroes' welcome by the American Zionist community. Glamorous, real-life pioneers, the two Bens, as they were referred to by their comrades, were fêted to a flurry of receptions, parties, and press conferences. For the next three years, Ben-Gurion traveled in America, speaking and writing about the rebirth of the Jewish homeland, attempting to recruit new pioneers for settlements in Palestine. His efforts at recruitment were somewhat disappointing, and he had signed up only 100 by 1916. But those who did join the cause were dedicated. One of the members won over by Ben-Gurion's enthusiasm was a young woman from Milwaukee named Goldie Mabovitch, who in later years, after changing her name to Golda Meir, became prime minister of Israel.

Ben-Gurion also collaborated with Ben-Zvi on several books about their experiences in Palestine, books intended to convince American Jews to support Zionism. The first book, entitled *Yizker* (*Commemoration*), chronicled the adventures of the Jewish watchmen in Palestine. The second, *Eretz Israel*, lovingly portrayed the land of their fathers to the Jewish masses in the United States. During his time in America, Ben-Gurion also became involved for the first time in the worldwide Zionist movement. He attended congresses and conferences, raised funds, and wrote and lectured for various publications. Ben-Gurion worked alongside several of the foremost leaders of the Zionist movement, who quickly realized that their young comrade had the makings of a political leader.

Ben-Gurion with his wife, Paula Munweiss, a Russian-Jewish nurse, shortly after their marriage in New York City on December 5, 1917. Though Paula loved David throughout their fifty years of marriage, she did not share his deep commitment to Zionism.

Soldiers of the Jewish Legion stand proudly before the sacred Wailing Wall in Jerusalem. The Jewish Legion, composed primarily of American and Palestinian Jews, was created by the British army in 1918 — partially in response to Ben-Gurion's lobbying — to help liberate Palestine from the Ottoman Empire.

> *I knew from the day that I met him that he was a great man. I could tell that he was like one of the prophets out of the Bible, a man of real vision.*
> —PAULA BEN-GURION
> on her husband

In his personal life Ben-Gurion was initially unhappy in New York. With only one close friend, Ben-Zvi, Ben-Gurion found New York to be intimidating and unfriendly. He wrote his childhood sweetheart, Rachel Nelkin, long, passionate letters begging her to leave everything to join him in America. But Rachel was married, and he could not turn the clock back.

In 1916 Ben-Gurion met Paula Munweiss at the house of a mutual friend. Short, with sad brown eyes and straight hair, Paula was not beautiful, but Ben-Gurion was charmed by her outspokenness and vitality. Though she had been dating a handsome young doctor for several years, she immediately took an interest in Ben-Gurion.

A year after they met Ben-Gurion proposed to Paula. He warned her that marriage would mean leaving the United States for a pioneer life of poverty "where there is no electricity, or gas, or electric trolleys." But she accepted anyway. Paula's job as a nurse and David's political activities precluded them from having a conventional ceremony. Instead they met at city hall in New York on the morning of December 5, 1917, and were married by a justice of the peace. As soon as the vows were exchanged, Ben-Gurion kissed his new bride on the cheek and hurried off to a political meeting.

Throughout his stay in the United States, Ben-Gurion had continually lobbied the British government to allow Jewish settlers in Palestine to fight alongside Allied troops against the Ottoman Empire. In February 1918 the British finally agreed to incorporate the Jewish Legion — many of whose members Ben-Gurion personally recruited — into a British army in the Middle East. In August 1918 Ben-Gurion landed in Egypt as a member of the 39th Royal Fusiliers. There he received a telegram from Paula informing him of the birth of their daughter Ge'ula, (a Hebrew name that translates as "liberation"). Ben-Gurion, so completely obsessed by his Zionist dream, even viewed this marvelous event in terms of politics. "The birth of our child," he wrote to Paula, "occurs at the happy moment when our land is being redeemed and the glory of this moment will light her entire life." In November 1919 David was reunited with Paula and their baby. Ben-Gurion was overjoyed, kissing and embracing his ecstatic wife and gently holding their child in his arms. Ben-Gurion would now devote his full energies toward building a Jewish homeland in Palestine.

THE ZIONIST ARCHIVE

Jewish Legion members in Egypt. Ben-Gurion joined the legion as a 32-year-old private in April 1918. He landed in Egypt in August, but before his battalion reached the front, the Turkish armies had collapsed.

3
Labor Zionism

After the war, Great Britain assumed control of Palestine. In doing so, it abandoned a promise it had made in the Sykes-Picot Agreement of 1916 to divide Palestine equally with France. British governance of the area received international sanction on April 25, 1920, at a meeting in San Remo, Italy, as the Supreme Council of Allied and Associated Powers officially divided up the Middle East into spheres of influence. While France received a mandate (responsibility for governing) for Lebanon, Syria, and Iraq, Britain was given a mandate for Palestine and Transjordan. The mandate for Palestine was later approved by the League of Nations on July 24, 1922.

Zionists were not sure how to react to the idea of British rule of Palestine. On the one hand, in 1915 Britain had promised Hussein, the sharif of Mecca, that an Arab homeland would be created in Palestine. On the other hand, on November 2, 1917, British Foreign Minister Arthur Balfour had sent a letter, known to history as the Balfour Declaration, to British Zionist leader Baron Lionel Walter Rothschild (the cousin of French Zionist leader Edmond de Rothschild) that pledged British support for "the establishment of a national home in Palestine for

> *The true right to a country — as to anything else — springs not from political or court authority, but from work.*
> —DAVID BEN-GURION

Ben-Gurion in the uniform of the Jewish Legion. At the end of World War I he returned to Palestine, which became the responsibility of Great Britain under a mandate from the League of Nations. His wife joined him there in November 1919.

THE ZIONIST ARCHIVE

> Foreign Office,
> November 2nd, 1917
>
> Dear Lord Rothschild,
>
> I have much pleasure in conveying to you, on behalf of His Majesty's Government, the following declaration of sympathy with Jewish Zionist aspirations which has been submitted to, and approved by, the Cabinet.
>
> "His Majesty's Government view with favour the establishment in Palestine of a national home for the Jewish people, and will use their best endeavours to facilitate the achievement of this object, it being clearly understood that nothing shall be done which may prejudice the civil and religious rights of existing non-Jewish communities in Palestine, or the rights and political status enjoyed by Jews in any other country"
>
> I should be grateful if you would bring this declaration to the knowledge of the Zionist Federation.

PICTURE PEOPLE

In November 1917 British foreign secretary Arthur Balfour sent this letter to Baron Lionel Walter Rothschild expressing his nation's support for a Jewish homeland in Palestine. The Balfour Declaration, as it was called, was an important symbolic gesture: it was the first time a sovereign government had formally endorsed the Zionist program.

the Jewish people." It had been an historic event: for the first time in history a sovereign nation had officially endorsed Zionism. The Declaration was widely acclaimed by Jews throughout the world. Though the short letter did not commit Britain to any practical measures, nor did it make clear what sort of "national home" the British envisioned — an autonomous nation, a province within an Arab country, or a federation with the Arabs — it was a gesture of great symbolic import.

But Ben-Gurion remained skeptical about British intentions. He acknowledged that Britain had indeed made a magnificent contribution to Zionism in recognizing the Jews' existence as a nation and their right to a homeland. But at the same time, he realized that because the Balfour Declaration was simply a symbolic demonstration of sympathy, Britain might easily abandon it if that proved expedient. Britain's conflicting loyalties to the Jews and the Arabs made this a real possibility.

Ultimately, Ben-Gurion decided that the question of whether Britain would lend support to the Zionist cause was secondary. Far more important than winning foreign support at this juncture, he argued, was establishing a stronger Jewish presence in Palestine. The Jews had barely begun to develop institutions for a national life and thus were not ready for statehood. Moreover, when they were ready, it would take more than British support. "Palestine," he wrote, "would not become ours through Great Britain giving her consent. Only the Hebrew people can transform this right into a tangible fact; only they, with body and soul, with their strength and capital, must build their national home." Jews, Ben-Gurion argued, had to increase their numbers in Palestine dramatically, to develop an economy, to create political institutions, and to strengthen defense organizations. Thus, the years after World War I became for Ben-Gurion years of work.

Ben-Gurion's emphasis on work over diplomacy brought him into conflict with Chaim Weizmann, who had become the leader of the World Zionist Organization after Herzl's death in 1904. Weizmann had become prominent by engineering the Balfour

Declaration. Along with Ben-Gurion he would dominate Zionism for the next 30 years. A world-renowned chemist (he discovered the formula for the manufacture of synthetic acetone, an important chemical in making ammunition), Weizmann was also a shrewd diplomat. During World War I, he had used his considerable charm, elegance, and wit to win the confidence of Britain's leading statesmen; the Balfour Declaration was the culmination of months of careful negotiation and lobbying. In keeping with the British tradition that he so respected, Weizmann believed the Jewish state could only be realized through painstaking diplomacy; the idea of creating a Jewish state through manual labor was, he felt, a utopian daydream. In 1921 Weizmann's opinion constituted the dominant policy of the World Zionist Organization, headquartered in London.

As Weizmann and Ben-Gurion argued over strategy during the 1920s, Jewish colonies grew substantially. By 1922, the year the League of Nations ratified Britain's mandate, there were 50 agricultural settlements in Palestine and the Jewish population had reached 100,000. Gradually, the institutions for national life that Ben-Gurion found so important were developing. There were political parties, labor unions, and schools. Hashomer, renamed *Haganah*, had become an unofficial army. Hebrew had become the main language of daily life. And under the terms of the British mandate, the Jews received their own quasigovernment, the Jewish Agency, which became responsible, as a subdivision of the British colonial administration, for Jewish development and activity.

Ben-Gurion believed that Weizmann's emphasis on diplomacy and negotiations ignored the potential of the Jewish workers in Palestine as a potent organizational and political force. He decided that he would harness this potential not only to make the Jewish community more powerful in Palestine but to attempt to gain control of the Zionist movement. When he proposed this to fellow laboring pioneers in Palestine, Ben-Gurion's comrades were astounded by his *chutzpah* (the Yiddish word for

AP/WIDE WORLD

Chaim Weizmann, the British scientist who developed TNT, assumed leadership of the Zionist movement after Theodor Herzl's death and secured the Balfour Declaration in 1917.

> *We shall gain Eretz Israel with labor, with capital, with culture, and with science.*
> —DAVID BEN-GURION

audacity). How, they asked, could a handful of pioneers in Palestine ever hope to accomplish such far-reaching aspirations?

The first step in Ben-Gurion's plan was to resolve the factional conflict between the Jewish labor parties in Palestine. In 1919 two rival labor parties merged into a new party, *Achdut ha-Avodah*; ten years later, this party would join hands with yet another labor party, *Hapoel Hatzair*, to form the *Mapai*. By 1929 the Mapai party would embrace 80 percent of all Jewish workers in Palestine and Ben-Gurion, the architect of the unification, would become the unquestioned leader of the party. Ben-Gurion was no longer a socialist, yet he remained committed to the primary tenet of socialist Zionism — that the working class would be the vanguard of the future Jewish homeland.

The second aspect of Ben-Gurion's scheme involved the organization known as *Histadrut* (General Federation of Hebrew Workers of the Land of Israel), which had been formed in 1920. Histadrut was then composed of only 4,500 workers out of a total population of 85,000 Jews in Palestine. The organization was unknown abroad and had few friends or financial benefactors. Yet Ben-Gurion, who held Histadrut membership card number three, was convinced that the organization could become the dominant force in the *Yishuv*, the Jewish community in Palestine. He would serve as

In 1924 Ben-Gurion laid the cornerstone for the Jerusalem headquarters of Histadrut, a federation of trade unions that he founded in 1920. Ben-Gurion believed that Jewish workers in Palestine should be the vanguard of Zionism.

leader of Histadrut for 15 years, from 1920 to 1935. These were to be years of tremendous challenges, but they were also the years in which Ben-Gurion was forged into a national leader.

Histadrut gradually became much more than a labor union. In addition to its labor organizing and political activities, it became one of the largest property owners in Palestine. It also owned retail outlets, construction companies, banks, newspapers, insurance companies, and a marketing network for agricultural produce. All were managed by the workers themselves. Indeed, the organization was dominated by a profound spirit of egalitarianism. The wages paid to the Histadrut managers were essentially the same as those paid to all workers. Eventually, Histadrut penetrated every sphere of life in the Yishuv; these institutions of Jewish life, exclusive of Arab and British control, were an indispensable feature of the struggle for a Jewish homeland.

Ben-Gurion's personal life suffered because of his single-minded obsession with politics. By 1925 Paula and he had had two more children, a son, Amos, and a daughter, Renana. Yet because of his busy schedule, Ben-Gurion had little time for his family. To his children, he seemed like a ghost. He showed little interest in their schoolwork or health and sometimes even had trouble recognizing them. His eldest daughter Ge'ula later wrote of her childhood: "We grew up at home as though we had no father." The burdens of bringing up the children, running the household, and managing the family finances fell unduly upon Paula.

Most of Ben-Gurion's spare time was spent reading and studying. Though his finances were usually in disarray, he always seemed to have enough money to buy books. He was the quintessential self-taught man. In order to read Plato in the original, he taught himself Greek. In order to prepare himself for becoming a leader in a future Jewish state, he studied Judaism, the history of the Middle East, the origins of Zionism, the history of the Arabs, countless books on statecraft, and memoirs of great leaders in history. Behind the brash, tempestuous

Workers learn new farming techniques at the Zionist School of Agriculture in Jerusalem in 1924.

exterior of the practical politician, there slowly emerged a man of broad learning with an unquenchable desire for knowledge. Yet in many ways Ben-Gurion still remained an enigma. He developed warm, long-lasting friendships, such as with Berl Katznelson, his lifelong friend and comrade in the Histadrut. At the same time he was a blunt, cold, often cruel man who would torment and challenge his friends just as viciously as his adversaries.

A familiar slogan of the first European Zionists had been "A people without a land returns to a land without a people." This was a common error of perception among most Europeans in the 19th and early 20th centuries. Palestine was anything but an empty land; the Jews were, until 1948, only a minority of the population. While the pioneers in Palestine, like Ben-Gurion, were aware that the Arab majority existed, they did not imagine that the Arabs had to be taken into consideration in forming a new nation. Labor Zionists believed they operated in a vacuum; until the bloody Arab riots of 1920, which left 135 Jews dead, they did not realize that the Palestinian Arabs also sought their own nation. Yet even then Zionist leaders tended to dismiss early Arab nationalism as merely the posturing of power-hungry, reactionary Arab leaders. The Arab masses, they argued, were motivated less by nationalist sentiments than by a desire to improve their material conditions. While the Zionists hoped for a Jewish national and social renaissance, they failed to realize that the Arabs of Palestine might hold similar aspirations.

Unlike Zionist extremists who called for the forcible expulsion of all Arabs from the future Jewish homeland, Ben-Gurion insisted that the two peoples could coexist peacefully. "A regime in Palestine," he wrote, "must at all times assure both the Jews and the Arabs the possibility of unhampered development and full national independence so as to rule out any domination by Arabs of Jews or Jews of Arabs." For the next decade, Ben-Gurion would be willing to consider a variety of compromise solutions to the Jewish-Arab dilemma, such as partition, federation, and a binational state. But in later years, the impact of Nazism and the rise in

> *Zionism is not founded on enmity.*
> —DAVID BEN-GURION

Ben-Gurion poses with his family: from left, son Amos, father Avigdor Green, daughters Ge'ula and Renana, and wife Paula. Ben-Gurion's political activities and incessant reading left him little time for his children, who often felt as if they had no father at all.

Though the first Zionist pioneers thought they were settling an empty land, in fact Palestine had long been inhabited by hundreds of thousands of Arabs, who themselves hoped to establish an independent nation. As late as 1914, Arabs outnumbered Jews in Palestine 10 to 1.

Arab violence would transform him into an uncompromising advocate of Zionist sovereignty.

During the 1920s, tensions between the two communities increasingly exploded into bloody conflict. In August 1929 Arab mobs launched attacks on Jewish settlements throughout Palestine; 133 Jews were killed, and 339 injured; 104 Arabs were killed by British army units used to control the outbursts. Although the immediate spark for the riots was a dispute between Jews and Arabs regarding worship practices at the Wailing Wall in Jerusalem, the underlying cause was Arab anxiety about increasing Jewish strength in Palestine.

The 1929 riots had a major impact on the political situation in Palestine. The British government wanted desperately to bring the conflict under control. A commission headed by Lord Passfield (Sidney James Webb) was sent to Palestine to investigate the causes and consequences of the riots. In November 1930 the commission issued a White Paper that was to serve as the basis for future British policy in Palestine. It proposed implementing severe restrictions on Jewish immigration and land purchases. Although Prime Minister Ramsay MacDonald disavowed the White Paper in 1931 after intense lobbying by Weizmann, Ben-Gurion believed the document demonstrated that Britain was beginning to have second thoughts about its commitment to the Zionist enterprise. If this were the case, Ben-Gurion asked, might not Weizmann's confidence in Britain be seriously misplaced?

Ben-Gurion decided that in 1930 the time had come to make a challenge for the leadership of the World Zionist Organization. Weizmann's position within Zionism had been severely undermined by the 1930 White Paper. His hold on the presidency of the World Zionist Organization seemed tenuous. The results of the Seventeenth Zionist Congress in July 1931 confirmed these suspicions. The labor faction led by Ben-Gurion emerged for the first time as the largest single group in the congress, with 29 percent of the delegates. Labor delegates captured two of the five seats on the Zionist executive board and Weizmann was defeated in the vote for president. Four years later, in 1935, the Labor slate won 44 percent of the delegates and Ben-Gurion was elected chairman of the Zionist executive board and appointed the head of the Jewish Agency. Ben-Gurion, at age 49, was now the unquestioned leader of Zionism.

AP/WIDE WORLD

Lord Passfield, the British colonial secretary who headed a commission sent to Palestine in 1929 to investigate the widespread Arab violence against Jewish settlements. His commission's final report, the White Paper of 1930, proposed limits on Jewish immigration and land purchases.

4
The Age of Nazism

In the latter half of the 1930s, Zionist leaders were distracted from affairs in Palestine by dark clouds threatening the fate of European Jewry. In 1935, two years after becoming ruler of Germany, Adolf Hitler enacted the Nuremberg Laws, which legalized discrimination against Jews in every walk of German life. On November 7, 1938, after a German diplomat in Paris was murdered by a 17-year-old Jewish refugee, violent mob attacks against Jews occurred throughout Germany. These infamous riots, referred to later as *Kristallnacht* (crystal night), became the first step in Hitler's diabolical plan to exterminate the European Jews. During the next two years thousands of Jewish shops and synagogues were burned; countless Jews were beaten and murdered; and more than 20,000 Jews were arrested and sent to concentration camps.

The Western powers, including both Great Britain and the United States, expressed sympathy for Jewish suffering, but closed their borders to Jewish immigration, except on a small scale. The rise of Nazism convinced Ben-Gurion more than ever that both the short-term and long-term salvation of the Jews lay in their own homeland. "It is not by caprice that the Jews return to Palestine," he argued, "for us it is a question of existence, of life and death."

> *The suspension of Jewish immigration will prove impossible without the aid of British bayonets.*
> —DAVID BEN-GURION

A Jewish couple walk hand-in-hand down a street in Berlin. Prominently displayed on their clothing are the yellow stars that all Jews in Adolf Hitler's Germany were forced to wear after September 1941. Each star bore the inscription *Jude*, the German word for Jew.

A crowd gathers outside a Jewish store damaged during the anti-Semitic riots that swept Germany on November 7, 1938 — the "crystal night." The violence added momentum to Hitler's campaign to rid Germany of Jewish influence.

After becoming leader of the Jewish Agency in 1935 (which essentially made him prime minister of the Jewish colonies in Palestine), Ben-Gurion began to search for a reconciliation with the Palestinian Arabs. In 1935 he held meetings with Musa Alami, a relative of the mufti of Jerusalem, the most respected Arab leader in Palestine. During their talks, Ben-Gurion proposed a daring solution to Arab-Jewish tensions. He suggested that the Jews be given an autonomous state within a larger federation of independent Arab states; Jews would be a majority in a tiny part of the federation, but Arabs would remain the overwhelming majority in the region. But Arab leaders rejected Ben-Gurion's overtures outright. They refused to agree in any way to the principle of a Jewish majority in Palestine.

When negotiations broke down temporarily, many resorted to violence. On April 19, 1936, Arab crowds rioted throughout Jaffa, knifing and shooting 16 Jews to death. Three days later, Arab leaders formed a Supreme Committee and began a general strike. They vowed to close down all shops, factories, and ports in Palestine until Great Britain stopped Jewish immigration, banned land sales to Jews, and granted Arabs in Palestine an independent state. For the next year, Palestine was a violent battleground. Arabs attacked Jewish colonies and buses and assassinated British police and officials. Great Britain eventually was forced to send in forces to crush the Arab revolt. In November, after Britain had instituted severe repressive measures, the Arabs ended the strike and disbanded the Supreme Committee.

Despite numerous provocations during the revolt, Ben-Gurion instructed the Jewish defense organization, the Haganah, which was formed after the 1921 riots, to adhere to a policy of *havlagah*, or self-restraint. Ben-Gurion was determined to let the British forces keep order, for he feared that any Jewish retaliation would lead to a full-scale civil war. Ironically, the Arab revolt helped give the Jewish economy a substantial boost. Because the Arab strike closed the Jaffa harbor, the Jews of Tel Aviv, two miles up the coast, received permission from the British to construct their own port.

British police clear the streets of Jaffa, Palestine's major port city, during the Arab rebellion of 1936. The rebellion included a general strike and a campaign of violence against Jewish settlements and British authorities.

The British were shocked by the Arab rebellion. In 1937 Great Britain formed another government commission to investigate the source of the disturbances and to recommend a permanent political settlement. After a series of hearings and conferences, the Peel Commission proposed a novel, radical solution: Palestine would be partitioned into two independent states, one Jewish, the other Arab. The Jewish state would occupy one fourth of the country; the Arabs would be given the rest of Palestine; areas of religious significance to both groups, such as Jerusalem and Bethlehem, would remain under British mandate.

The Arabs objected to partition of any sort; they felt it violated their unalienable rights to the land of Palestine. The majority of the Jewish community likewise rejected the plan; Ben-Gurion, however, presciently realized the true potential of the scheme. Ben-Gurion argued that the proposed partial Jewish state would only be a beginning. Over time, he argued, the Jews would be able to acquire the country in its entirety. To his mind, the threat of Hitler's Nazi Germany to Jews in Europe made it especially

> *The area offered [the Jews] was so restricted as to make impossible the emergence of a viable Jewish state.*
> —MAURICE EDELMAN
> British historian, on the Peel Commission's plan of partition

important to make a start. Ben-Gurion said he was "moved to the depths of my heart and the chasm of my soul by the great and wonderful redeeming vision of the Jewish state whose hour has pealed." The World Zionist Organization, however, rejected Ben-Gurion's recommendations and voted against partition.

The debate in 1937 over partition, which would be replayed a decade later, neatly encapsulated the immense difficulties in reaching a peaceful settlement in Palestine. The Arabs believed Palestine was theirs because they had lived on the land for centuries; the Jews believed they had an historic birthright to Israel. The Arabs saw Jewish immigration as the invasion of alien forces; for the Jews it was a return to their own country after centuries of forced separation. "Both we and they want to be in the majority," Ben-Gurion lamented. "The only question was whether this tragic clash could be played out without bloodshed." History resolved Ben-Gurion's uncertainty: violence became an inevitable legacy of these irreconcilable differences.

The shifting terrain of global politics now contributed to a change in Great Britain's policy in the Middle East. The French Third Republic was collapsing and Nazi Germany was ominously threatening the rest of Europe with its newly developed military strength. In Munich in 1938 British Prime Minister Neville Chamberlain, in a futile attempt to prevent war, appeased Hitler in his demand for control of Czechoslovakia. Britain would henceforth view the Palestine problem in terms of short-term strategic interests. Great Britain needed to ensure the friendship and loyalty of Arab countries in the Middle East in order to safeguard essential naval bases and routes in case war broke out. The British feared the Arabs might ally themselves with Germany and Italy against Britain and her allies.

The British government accordingly announced in 1939 that it would no longer be bound by the Balfour Declaration. The British issued another White Paper in May, proposing the establishment of an independent state with an Arab majority within ten years. They also imposed severe restric-

> *For the first time in nearly two thousand years a defense force has been established which is Jewish, for a Jewish reason, to protect the Jewish population.*
> —DAVID BEN-GURION
> on the establishment of the *Haganah*

DAVID BEN-GURION CENTENNIAL COMMISSION

tions on Jewish land purchases and placed a quota on immigration of 75,000 people over the next five years; after the five-year period, further immigration would be subject to Arab consent. This White Paper would guide British policy in Palestine until the establishment of the Jewish state in 1948.

On September 1, 1939, Adolf Hitler's troops invaded Poland and the horrors of World War II began. Ben-Gurion wrote Paula of his suspicions of what lay ahead, "I can foresee global cataclysms that will turn the earth almost upside down." The Nazi blitzkrieg steamrolled over France in the spring of 1940 and Great Britain suddenly found itself on the front lines of the war.

Ben-Gurion arrived in the United States in 1941 to mobilize American Jews in support of establishing a Jewish homeland in Palestine after the war. In May 1942 he helped organize the first national

Ben-Gurion (center, front row) and other Zionist leaders at an Arab-Jewish peace conference in London in 1939. Britain, which needed the support of Arab countries during World War II, eventually abandoned such negotiations and issued the 1939 White Paper, which severely restricted Jewish immigration to Palestine.

A Jewish state in part of Palestine would help in the realization of Zionism more than a British state over the whole of Palestine.
—DAVID BEN-GURION

51

With Hermann Göring directly behind him, Adolf Hitler addresses the German *Reichstag*, or parliament, in 1940. Hitler's extermination of 6 million Jews in concentration camps throughout Europe, known as the Holocaust, reduced the Jewish population worldwide by almost 50 percent.

conference of American Jewry in New York City. Called the Biltmore Conference, it was an historic occasion: for the first time, Zionists agreed to a resolution that unequivocally supported the establishment of a Jewish state in Palestine. Though this had been the goal of Zionism for years, leaders had avoided stating it publicly so as not to jeopardize foreign support. The conference represented a triumph of Ben-Gurion's militant policies over Weizmann's moderate approach.

Ben-Gurion returned to Palestine in 1942 to discover that the British continued to apply the White Paper restrictions. Palestine remained closed to the handful of refugees who were fortunate enough to escape the Nazi terror. British patrol boats stopped a number of ships loaded with refugees and forced them to head back to occupied Europe. The British also cracked down on the Haganah, forbidding Jews from carrying weapons in public. When Ben-Gurion protested that Jews had the right to arm themselves in self-defense, his pleas were ignored. The dilemma for Jews was how to oppose effectively British policy in Palestine without undermining the war against Nazi Germany.

Some Jews attempted to drive the British out of Palestine through terrorism. Two main terrorist groups developed, the *Lehi* and the *Irgun*. (The latter was led by future Prime Minister Menachem Begin.) Members of these groups indiscriminately shot British policemen, bombed jails, and in 1944, assassinated Lord Moyne, a British minister in Palestine. Ben-Gurion forthrightly condemned the extremists and urged the Jewish community to refuse them shelter. At his behest, the Haganah handed over Irgun terrorists directly to the British. Though Ben-Gurion was not fond of Great Britain, he felt that terrorism hindered the effort to defeat Nazi Germany — which took precedence over all other concerns.

The defeat of Germany became an even more pressing concern to Zionist leaders when they learned of Hitler's "final solution." Hitler was now attempting the wholesale extermination of Jews throughout the continent. In concentration camps at Auschwitz and Treblinka and other places millions of Jews had been killed. Jews in Palestine were filled with horror and overcome by a feeling of helplessness. The United States and Great Britain ignored appeals by American Jews and other Zionists to try to rescue the European Jews and refused to bomb the concentration camps or the railroads leading to them. The desire to gain Allied support for Jewish independence restrained the Zionists from launching any independent operations to free Jews from the camps. By the end of the war, the immense tragedy of the Holocaust had killed 6 million Jews.

During the war, Ben-Gurion's friends referred to him as the "Old Man." According to most stories, the custom originated when he was eating in a restaurant with some friends. A young girl at a nearby table pointed at Ben-Gurion and loudly asked her parents, "Who is that old man?" To the delight of Ben-Gurion's friends, the nickname stuck, even though Ben-Gurion was only in his fifties: he was now the most respected leader of the Zionist movement. His speeches and writings were avidly bought and studied by Jews throughout the world. But his personality had not changed. He was still completely consumed by his work, rarely taking time out to relax.

Ben-Gurion was in London when British Prime Minister Winston Churchill announced Germany's surrender on May 8, 1945. Londoners jammed the streets, singing and cheering. For Ben-Gurion, victory was bittersweet; he could not block out the memory of the millions of Jews who perished in Hitler's death camps. After the war, he visited the camps. There he saw firsthand the horrible destructiveness of the Nazi terror. Ben-Gurion was mobbed by Jewish refugees eager to meet and touch the Zionist leader. Tears poured down his face as he promised them that a Jewish state would soon await them in Palestine. "During those six years of war, we never forgot you for a single day," Ben-Gurion declared. "We have been working to build up our land so that you may come there to live as decent human beings again among your own people and where you will not fear again." Three long years were to pass before Ben-Gurion's promise could be fulfilled.

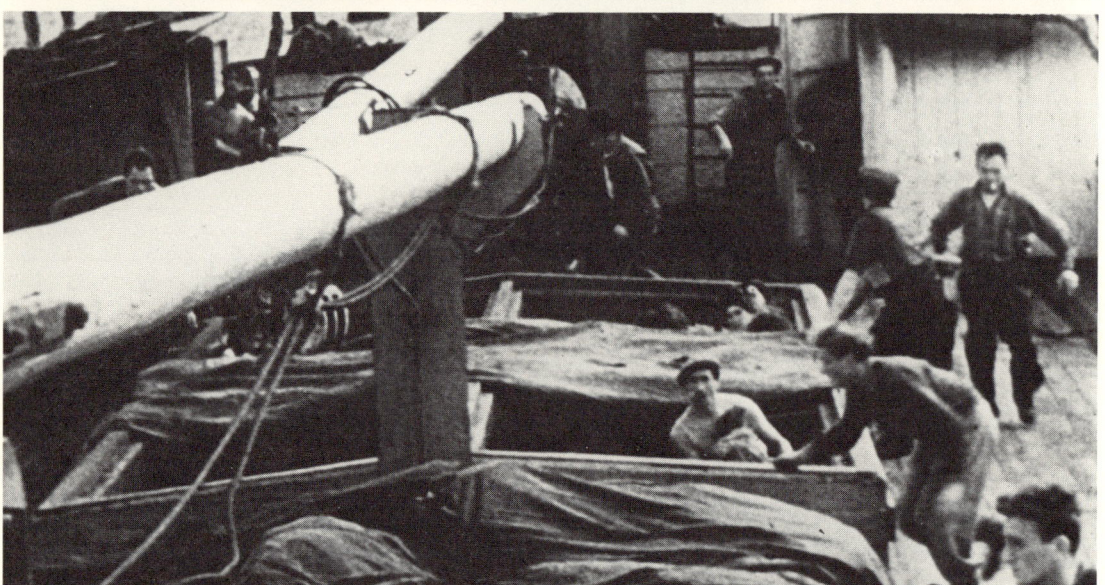

5
The Division of Palestine

With the horrors of the Holocaust now dramatically revealed to the world, support for a Jewish state in Palestine acquired international legitimacy. The sight of hundreds of thousands of Holocaust survivors jammed into squalid refugee camps across Europe provided substantial proof of the vital need for a Jewish homeland. Harry Truman, who became the U.S. president after the death of Franklin D. Roosevelt in 1945, pledged his administration's support for the Zionist cause.

In Britain the rise to power of the Labour party, under the leadership of Clement Attlee, in 1945 seemed to promise additional gains for the Zionist movement. During the war, the Labour leaders had opposed the White Paper restrictions and promised that, if elected, a Labour administration would seek the establishment of a Jewish state. Ben-Gurion, normally skeptical of British promises, uncharacteristically applauded Labour's victory: "The British workers," he wrote, "will understand our aims." The Yishuv was no longer a minority settlement: the Jewish population had reached 560,000 by 1944, and the Jewish economy was prospering. Indeed, the momentum for a Jewish state now seemed undeniable.

> There is no common ground between them.... Their cultural and social life, their ways of thought and conduct, are as incompatible as their national aspirations.
> —report of the Peel Commission on the Arabs and the Jews in Palestine

Jewish refugees en route to Palestine clear the decks of their ship to avoid detection by a British plane. The many ramshackle vessels that ferried Jewish refugees from Europe to Palestine after the war were forced to brave a British naval blockade.

UPI/BETTMANN NEWSPHOTOS

Ernest Bevin, British foreign secretary, directed his nation's strict enforcement of the 1939 White Paper quotas on Jewish immigration to Palestine. Under Bevin, Britain imposed curfews in Palestine, imprisoned Jewish resistance leaders, and seized Jewish refugee ships.

> The best mandatory government in the world is not to be compared with a government of our own.
> —DAVID BEN-GURION

Ten days after Clement Attlee's succession to power, Ben-Gurion led a delegation to London to meet with Ernest Bevin, Great Britain's new foreign secretary. Ben-Gurion requested that 100,000 Jewish refugees in Europe be allowed to emigrate immediately to Palestine; he also asked that the White Paper restrictions be completely abolished. The Zionist leadership was dumbfounded and appalled when Bevin announced several weeks later that not only would the British government continue to enforce the White Paper restrictions but that the Labour party had withdrawn its support for a Jewish state in Palestine.

The Labour government's shift in policy was a consequence of the strategic predicament that Great Britain faced after the war. World War II had left the country virtually bankrupt. The new Labour government, which planned ambitious social welfare programs, needed to ensure control over its single most important overseas resource, oil. Britain's resources of petroleum were concentrated in the Middle East. The safety of these holdings depended on maintaining friendly relations with Arab nations, which would be jeopardized if Great Britain permitted extensive Jewish immigration into Palestine.

Ernest Bevin's personal beliefs were also instrumental in this shift in policy. He regarded the Jewish refugees the same way as he did other European war victims and objected to any favorable treatment for the Jews. "If the Jews, with all their suffering, want to get too much at the head of the queue," Bevin warned, "you have the danger of another anti-Semitic reaction."

Bevin's intransigence on immigration forced Ben-Gurion to approve a campaign of armed resistance against the British. In October 1945 he authorized the Haganah to develop an alliance with their former antagonists, the Irgun and the Lehi. Though Ben-Gurion did not believe the Jews could drive the British out of Palestine through armed resistance, he did think that terrorism might lead to an excessive British reaction that could improve Zionism's appeal worldwide. For the next eight months Zionist forces launched systematic attacks on the British military establishment. The Haganah liberated several hundred illegal Jewish immigrants from British detention camps, destroyed British ships used for intercepting refugee vessels, sabotaged radar stations and lighthouses, and dynamited railway installations. Shortly after midnight on June 17, 1946, the Haganah launched their most daring attack, destroying Palestine's 11 major bridges.

Less than two weeks later the British mounted a furious counterattack. On Saturday, June 29, thereafter referred to as "Black Saturday" by the Jews of Palestine, the British mobilized 17,000 troops and several hundred tanks and armored cars. The borders were closed, a curfew was imposed throughout the country, and leaders of the Jewish Agency were arrested. (Ben-Gurion was in Paris, luckily.)

Britain's attempts to intimidate the Yishuv and destroy the Haganah were largely unsuccessful and instead provoked a vicious retaliation by Zionist extremists. In July 1946 Irgun forces planted a bomb in the southern wing of Jerusalem's King

> *We reject the infamy of assailing an Arab just because he is one. We will not play the terrorists' beastly game.*
> —DAVID BEN-GURION
> attacking the policies of the Irgun

Palestinian police carry the body of a Jewish immigrant killed by British naval personnel during the seizure of the refugee ship *Theodor Herzl* off the Palestinian seacoast. Ben-Gurion responded to a wave of such killings in 1946 by ordering the Jewish underground militia to carry out a clandestine war against British authorities.

Protesting Britain's opposition to Jewish immigration to Palestine, some 30,000 men and women marched through Philadelphia in November 1946. Britain's harsh policy was intended to cultivate friendly relations with Arab nations in order to safeguard precious Middle Eastern oil reserves.

> We must make the Jews who come back home proud that they are Jews.
>
> —DAVID BEN-GURION

David Hotel, which then housed the British mandatory offices. Ninety people died and hundreds were injured in the blast. Ben-Gurion denounced the attack and ordered the Jewish community to assist the British police in apprehending the perpetrators.

The King David attack precipitated a major change in Ben-Gurion's strategy. As Zionist moderates formed a coalition to oppose Zionist militancy, Ben-Gurion instructed the Haganah to halt the armed struggle. Instead, he committed all of the Yishuv's underground forces to a massive clandestine operation aimed at smuggling Jews into Palestine. Zionist operatives purchased dilapidated, barely seaworthy boats and developed inventive ways of slipping past the British blockade. In late 1946, in response to this campaign, Great Britain intensified its offshore patrols. It began to intercept the majority of the refugee ships. When one ship was towed into Haifa harbor, its passengers unfurled a banner over the deck: "We survived Hitler," the banner proclaimed, "death is no stranger to us.

Nothing can keep us from our Jewish homeland. The blood be on your head if you fire on this unarmed vessel." Pictures of this boat and others, filled to the brim with refugees desperate for freedom, profoundly stirred the sympathies of western audiences.

Ben-Gurion renewed his quest for a negotiated solution in 1947. In private talks with Bevin, Ben-Gurion suggested the possibility of establishing a Jewish state within which Britain could maintain a network of military bases and retain oil drilling rights in the southern Palestinian desert. Ben-Gurion hoped that Great Britain, with its strategic concerns thus allayed, would reconsider its attitude toward the Zionists. But Bevin refused to agree to a Jewish state of any kind.

The impossibility of a compromise settlement and the increasingly heavy costs of maintaining Britain's military presence in Palestine drove Bevin, in 1947, to refer the entire Palestine problem to the newly formed United Nations. The challenge of satisfying the legitimate aspirations to statehood of two bitterly hostile communities seemed perfectly suited to the mission of the UN. On May 13, 1947, an 11-nation investigative board, the United Nations Special Committee on Palestine (UNSCOP), was formed. In hearings before the Committee in Palestine, Ben-Gurion presented the Zionist case. "Can the consciousness of humanity," he asked, "absolve itself of all responsibility for the Holocaust? There is only one security guarantee: a homeland and a state."

Ben-Gurion's argument was dramatically reinforced by the plight of the refugees on the ship *Exodus*. A run-down ferry packed with 4,500 Holocaust survivors, the *Exodus* attempted to crack the blockade but was intercepted by British ships, which began escorting it toward Palestine. Twelve miles offshore, fighting broke out between the British forces and the refugees. The British navy opened fire with machine guns, killing 3 and wounding 100. A detailed account of the battle was radioed to Haganah headquarters and then rebroadcast to an incredulous world audience. Members of UNSCOP

> *The Bevin policy is a clear attempt to do away with the Jews as a nation and to recognize the existence only of dispersed Jewish communities, to be either objects of charity to other peoples, or targets for their pogroms.*
> —DAVID BEN-GURION

Jewish youths drive triumphantly through the streets of Tel Aviv in November 1947, celebrating the United Nations' decision to divide Palestine into separate Jewish and Arab states.

were horrified when after the *Exodus* docked in Haifa its passengers were forced to board British prison ships sailing back to Europe.

The committee published its recommendations several days after the *Exodus* tragedy. They proposed a partition of Palestine into separate Arab and Jewish states with Jerusalem placed under international supervision. The partition plan was a mapmaker's nightmare, but Ben-Gurion felt it was the best possible compromise. Not only would a Jewish state in half of Palestine provide immediate refuge for the Jews still trapped in Europe, it would also consolidate the strong institutions in the Yishuv, which the Labor Zionists had so painstakingly created. Under the UNSCOP plan, the Jewish state would represent 55 percent of the land, with a citizenry 58 percent Jewish; the Arab state would acquire 45 percent of Palestine, with a population 98 percent Arab. The Committee recognized that both sides possessed equally valid yet apparently irreconcilable claims to Palestine and they hoped that partition would prove to be a just settlement. The Committee anticipated that there would be considerable animosity and suspicion at first, but they believed over time a peaceful understanding would evolve between the two nations.

Ben-Gurion and the Zionists supported the partition plan, but it was unanimously rejected by all the Arab nations. Indeed, the Arab League formally threatened war if the UN approved the UNSCOP report. But on November 29, 1947, with support from both the United States and the Soviet Union, the UN General Assembly voted for partition: the British mandate would end on May 14, 1948. "That night, crowds danced in the street," recalled Ben-Gurion. "I could not dance. I knew that we faced war and that in it we would lose the best of our youth."

UPI/BETTMANN NEWSPHOTOS

Ben-Gurion and Golda Meir exchange congratulations on the passage of the UN partition plan on November 29, 1947. The plan paved the way for the creation of an independent Jewish state, something that had not existed for more than 2,000 years.

6
The Soldier

For years before the partition of Palestine Ben-Gurion had believed that a military conflict with the Arabs was inevitable. In 1946 he had asked the Jewish Agency to appoint him as defense minister in Palestine. Ben-Gurion's comrades were skeptical that, as a political leader with virtually no military experience, he could suddenly transform himself into a military strategist. But they underestimated Ben-Gurion's abilities.

After being appointed defense minister, Ben-Gurion immersed himself in military matters with his usual zeal. His study room was soon strewn with maps, charts, and piles of books about famous military campaigns. Haganah commanders in Palestine were summoned to appear at Ben-Gurion's "seminars" where they were interrogated at length by the "Old Man" on every imaginable military topic.

Ben-Gurion's initial investigations into the strength of his army were disheartening. To the rest of the world, the reputation of the Haganah had reached legendary proportions. During the Jews' war for statehood, the British had estimated Jewish forces at 80,000 men. The reality was considerably less impressive. The Haganah had only 40,000 reserves, and they were poorly equipped and had min-

> *There are many like me in Israel, of the stuff no terror weakens.*
> —DAVID BEN-GURION

Ben-Gurion and Brigadier Yigael Yadin observe Israeli army maneuvers. Anticipating an eventual armed struggle with the Arabs, Ben-Gurion secured appointment in 1946 as defense minister of the Jewish Agency and set about strengthening Jewish military forces.

AP/WIDE WORLD

> *The Englishman does not see things through Jewish eyes, he does not feel with a Jewish heart, and he does not reason with a Jewish brain.*
>
> —DAVID BEN-GURION

Troops of the Arab Liberation Army guard their position at a crossroad in April 1948. Between November 1947, when Palestine was partitioned, and May 1948, when Israel was established, Palestinian Jews and Arabs fought several skirmishes — an irregular war without fixed front lines.

imal training and little experience. The only fully mobilized force was the 3,000 member *Palmach*, an elite unit of the Haganah that had been formed from kibbutz settlements in 1941 in order to protect Jewish villages against a potential German attack. The Palmach had collaborated with the British army during World War II, embarking on joint raids and intelligence missions.

Five months before the UN's historic decision, Ben-Gurion gathered all the Haganah commanders together in his Tel Aviv home. He told them that the Yishuv must prepare for a war. "There is going to be a war," Ben-Gurion declared. "There will be battlefronts. This will no longer be a war of platoons or sections. It is essential to set up a modern army." His commanders sat in stunned silence. Indeed, they wondered if the "Old Man" had lost his mind. The commanders felt that at the most the partition would bring flurries of guerrilla fighting resembling the Arab revolt of 1936. Thus, the Haganah and Palmach saw no need for heavy weaponry or for a change in tactics.

Ben-Gurion refused to change his mind. The Yishuv had to be prepared for a conventional fight and

the Haganah had to be converted into a regular army with heavy weapons. Ben-Gurion, against Haganah objections, also insisted on a major strategic decision. In case of war the Haganah must be prepared to defend every Jewish settlement in the Yishuv. No settlement, no matter how isolated, would be abandoned even if it was located within the boundaries of the proposed Arab state. Furthermore, Ben-Gurion stated that if the Arab states insisted on going to war, then the Jewish state would no longer be obligated to respect the boundaries drawn up by the UN plan. The frontiers of the Jewish state would be those that its army could seize.

As Ben-Gurion predicted, the Arabs responded to the UN support of partition with violence. Three hundred Jewish homes and eleven synagogues were burned to the ground in Syria; similar incidents occurred in several Arab countries. Attacks in Palestine began almost immediately. The morning after the UN vote, four Jewish passengers were attacked on a Jerusalem bus; a few days later five Jews were killed in broad daylight in the Arab city of Ramla. Arab attacks were immediately answered by reprisals from Irgun and Haganah forces. Fighting slowly evolved into an irregular war without stationary front lines. Battles raged around isolated outposts, in suburbs, or on highways as each side attempted to capture as much territory as possible before the British departed. British troops were often openly sympathetic to the Arab cause. Winston Churchill, in temporary retirement, accused Bevin of conducting a "dirty war" against the Jews of Palestine. On several occasions British soldiers disarmed Haganah fighters and then handed them over to Arab mobs, which brutally murdered them.

In January 1948 the Arab Legion (Transjordan's army, which had been trained by the British) began a siege of the Jewish quarter in the old city of Jerusalem. The blockade focused on the single road, full of twisting curves and perilous cliffs, that linked Jerusalem to western Palestine. By the early months of 1948, the Arab Legion had completely closed off the road. Ben-Gurion suggested a daring plan to break the siege. He proposed that the Haganah forgo

AP/WIDE WORLD

Black clouds from a burning Arab movie theater fill the sky over a troubled Jerusalem. The fire was set by Jews in December 1948 in retaliation for Arab attacks that followed the UN partition announcement.

> *He influenced through the force of his personality no less than through his doctrines.*
> —MOSHE DAYAN on Ben-Gurion

its normal underground tactics and for the first time operate openly in full strength toward the single objective of freeing Jerusalem. He called for 1,800 of the Haganah's best troops to be mobilized from around the country, though this would mean every other front in the country would be critically exposed to attack. Such an operation promised to be a desperate gamble, but a forceful Ben-Gurion persuaded the Zionist cabinet to accept the risky proposal.

The plan was christened Operation Nachshon after the first Jew who, according to legend, marched into the parting waters of the Red Sea during the flight from Egypt. It was deceptively simple. The Arab towns dominating the vital crossing would be captured and Jewish forces would temporarily establish a safe corridor on both sides of the road. The offensive began on April 3, 1948, with an assault on the mountain fortress of Kastel, five miles east of Jerusalem. Despite fierce resistance, enough of the road was secured to enable the first convoy of 250 vehicles to pass through to Jerusalem. When

An Arab family flees Jaffa in 1948. The marked expansion of Jewish territory during the irregular war of 1947–48 uprooted more than 400,000 Arabs from their villages in Palestine.

In July 1948 Ben-Gurion and his wife bid an official farewell to the last British soldiers to leave the Holy Land. In the months following the 1947 UN partition vote, approximately 100,000 British troops, police, and civilians were evacuated from Palestine.

news of the convoy reached the city, hundreds of Jewish residents jammed the streets to greet their saviors. Children climbed up onto the trucks with flowers in their hands and young women jumped onto running boards to kiss the heroic drivers.

Although the road to Jerusalem had only been opened for a few days, Operation Nachshon was considered the turning point in the irregular war, giving Jerusalem enough supplies to enable it to withstand several prolonged sieges. Many historians consider it the most important operation in the War of Independence. The campaign was an immense personal triumph for Ben-Gurion, marking his coming-of-age as a daring military leader.

Meanwhile, the Arabs were being torn apart by historic, tribal, national, and personal rivalries. The principal leader of the Palestinian Arabs, the mufti of Jerusalem, Haj Amin al-Husseini, who was wary of any threat to his personal authority, refused to cooperate with the other major Arab Palestinian army, the Arab Army of Liberation in Galilee, or with other Arab nations. At the same time, King Abdullah of Transjordan revealed his desire to annex the entire Arab area of partitioned Palestine to his own domain. Arab armies also were handicapped by inexperience, low morale, and corruption and incompetence among their leaders. Despite occasional

American Jewish children celebrate the birth of Israel on May 14, 1948, by dancing the Hora, a Jewish folk dance, outside the offices of the Jewish Agency in Washington, D.C. Above them hangs the flag of the new nation. Similar celebrations took place in Jewish communities throughout the world.

Arab victories, a defeatist attitude swept the Arab ranks. During the spring of 1948, a mass exodus of Arabs from Jewish-controlled areas of Palestine took place. On April 9, 1948, units of the Irgun and Lehi captured the Arab village of Deir Yassin. More than 200 Arab men, women, and children were killed in the attack and their bodies were mutilated by the Jewish soldiers. Afterward, thousands of Arab peasants, afraid of continued terrorist attacks, fled their villages. By May 1948, more than 400,000 Arabs had left their homes in Palestine, never to return.

As May 14 (the date on which British forces were scheduled to leave Palestine) grew closer, Arab nations continued to threaten a full-scale invasion against the Jews unless the partition plan was overturned. Ben-Gurion and the other Jewish leaders debated an appropriate course of action. In April 1948 the National Council had been formed under Ben-Gurion's leadership to replace the Jewish Agency as the primary body responsible for Jewish affairs in Palestine. Members of the council gathered on May 12 to discuss whether the Zionists should proclaim a Jewish state two days hence. Golda Meir had just returned from a secret trip to Transjordan, where she had met with King Abdullah in a last-minute attempt at peaceful compromise. Although the meeting had been cordial, Meir reported that no settlement had been realized.

Moshe Sharett had met the day before with U.S. Secretary of State George Marshall, who had expressed his desire to suspend partition and place Palestine under an indefinite UN trusteeship until a new settlement could be reached. Sharett told the National Council that the United States probably would not provide aid to the Jewish state if the Arabs invaded. Yigael Yadin, the Haganah's chief of operations, estimated that Jewish chances of victory in a war were at best 50-50. Some committee members wavered in their support for an immediate proclamation and recommended that the Zionists accept the U.S. truce proposal.

Ben-Gurion had no such misgivings: he felt the Jews should risk everything and proclaim the state. Any hesitation might well prove fatal, he told other members of the National Council, because the UN could use the delay to reconsider the Palestinian question. His own military experts notwithstanding, Ben-Gurion felt the superior determination and willpower of the Jewish community would provide the crucial edge in the war. He confidently declared, "I dare believe in victory. We shall triumph."

> *[The convoy] was the first indication that as a military leader he could show the same power of decision, the same ruthlessness, and the same imagination, as he had shown in the political struggle.*
> —BARNET LITVINOFF
> British historian, on Ben-Gurion

7
War of Independence

After the dramatic Proclamation of Independence of the State of Israel on May 14, 1948, Ben-Gurion, as head of the National Council, became leader of the new country. Within hours of taking power, he was informed by Haganah commanders that the armies of five Arab nations — Egypt, Transjordan, Syria, Iraq, and Lebanon — were attacking on all fronts. The Arabs expected the invasion to be an easy mop-up operation, requiring only a few days to complete. Although the size of the opposing armies was roughly equivalent, the Arabs enjoyed much greater firepower than the Israelis, who were helpless to match the tanks, artillery, and aircraft of the Arab armies.

Hostilities began when Egyptian planes launched a bombing raid on Tel Aviv shortly after midnight on May 14. Ben-Gurion, who had just finished a radio broadcast to the people of the United States, hurried off to inspect the damage, driving unescorted in an open jeep. He later recalled; "From all the houses, people in pajamas and night gowns were gazing out, but there were no signs of panic. I felt that these people would stand their ground."

> *How beautiful is this day, May 14th, when the whole world is holding its breath anticipating the entry of seven Arab armies into Palestine to redeem it from the Zionists and the West.*
> —from the diary of an Arab Legion officer, May 14, 1948

Israeli air force mechanics salvage machine guns from a downed Egyptian fighter plane during the 1948–49 Arab-Israeli war, which began on May 15, 1948, the day after the establishment of Israel. In combating an invasion by five Arab states, Israel initially had very few weapons.

AP/WIDE WORLD

The most revered military leader in the history of Israel, Moshe Dayan takes a break from maneuvers in Gaza in 1948 to share lunch with his troops. After serving as a lieutenant colonel in the War of Independence, Dayan became chief of staff of the Israeli army and directed his nation to victories in the 1956 Sinai campaign and the 1967 Six-Day War.

At the outset, Ben-Gurion's objective was to stall for time. Israel had purchased heavy arms (including tanks, planes, and artillery) from Czechoslovakia and France but they were not expected to be delivered for several weeks.

Yigal Allon, the young Palmach commander, remarked that the new state of Israel resembled "a nude girl with only a handkerchief to cover herself." Israeli forces were thinly spread across the country, respecting Ben-Gurion's strategy that every Jewish settlement within Palestine should be protected. In a matter of days, the Egyptians penetrated to within 25 miles of Tel Aviv, the capital of the new state. At the same time, troops from Transjordan's Arab Lecut across the middle of Israel, threatening to cut the nation in half. Jerusalem, which lay isolated in an area dominated by the Arabs, was being bombarded ferociously.

The first real crisis occurred in Galilee, a region in the north of Israel. On May 18, 1948, a Syrian column of 200 armored vehicles, including 45 tanks, stormed Degania, the oldest kibbutz in Palestine. The beleaguered defenders attempted to stall the Syrians' advance with homemade bombs and Molotov cocktails, but they knew that without artillery or reinforcements, they would soon have to evacuate the settlement. Ben-Gurion ordered two antiquated 65-millimeter cannons, representing half of Israel's total artillery, to be rushed to Degania. The local commander, Lieutenant Colonel Moshe Dayan, later Israel's minister of defense, deployed the cannons at the same moment the first Syrian tanks pierced the kibbutz perimeter. The Israelis scored a direct hit on the tanks and the Syrians, unaware that the obsolete weapons were the only arms the Israelis had, broke off their attack and retreated back into the hills.

During the first month of fighting the key area was Jerusalem. Throughout the first three and a half weeks of the war, the Jewish area of Jerusalem was constantly bombarded by Arab heavy artillery. Ten thousand shells were fired, destroying more than two thousand homes. Food and drinking water were sharply rationed. As Arab forces intensified their attack, the prospect of mass starvation became quite real. Against the objections of the general staff, Ben-Gurion insisted that full military priority be given to opening the road to Jerusalem. "I knew," he would later recall, "that if ever the people of the country saw Jerusalem fall, they would lose their faith."

The operation would require a frontal assault on the Latrun, a police fortress located high on the cliffs above the Jerusalem road. Because the Haganah had only a single, sorely depleted brigade available for the attack, Ben-Gurion went to the Tel Aviv docks to recruit personally some new soldiers. He convinced hundreds of immigrants on a ship that

> *Jews will sacrifice themselves for Jerusalem no less than Englishmen for London, Russians for Moscow, or Americans for Washington.*
> —DAVID BEN-GURION

had just arrived in Israel to risk their lives to defend their new homeland. Most of the men had never before held a rifle.

Just past midnight on an eerily quiet evening, the newly reinforced brigade opened its assault on Latrun. As the Jewish troops took up positions across the picturesque wheat fields beneath the fortress, they were somehow spotted by Arab watchmen. The element of surprise was lost. The Arabs responded with a horrifying barrage of artillery and machine-gun fire that trapped many of the Israelis where they stood. Many of the raw immigrant recruits panicked, broke off the attack, and as they fled down the hill became easy marks for Arab sharpshooters. Ultimately, the assault was a disaster, as the Jews suffered more than 200 casualties — the bloodiest defeat an Israeli unit has ever suffered in four wars with the Arabs. Ben-Gurion insisted on further attacks against the fortress but three more assaults by Israeli forces were repulsed with heavy losses. Latrun threatened to become, in Ben-Gurion's words, the "graveyard of Jewish hopes for breaking the siege of Jerusalem."

However, two Palmach scouts, attempting to find an alternative route to Jerusalem, accidentally dis-

Jewish soldiers take over an Arab village in June 1948. During the first month of the war, the Israelis carried out few such offensives, opting instead for a defensive posture until additional arms could be acquired from foreign allies.

UPI/BETTMANN NEWSPHOTOS

covered a little-used shepherds' path on the steep slopes in the mountains surrounding the city. The rocky road bypassed Latrun and ran exclusively through Israeli territory. Ben-Gurion ordered the Haganah to build a paved road along the shepherds' path that could accomodate large supply trucks. Equipped with only chisels, wooden hammers, and shovels, an army of laborers feverishly constructed the "Burma Road" (as the roadway was nicknamed after the famous supply route that connected Burma to China during World War II). Arab peasants reported that the Jews were building a secret route to Jerusalem, but the Arab commander in the area discounted the reports. "The terrain is too tough," he said, "they will never get a road through there." At one stretch, a steep ravine of three miles separated the end of the "Burma Road" from the last point trucks could reach from Jerusalem. Hundreds of citizens from Tel Aviv were mobilized to carry supplies and equipment by hand up and down the makeshift route. Usually working at night without the benefit of flashlights, the volunteers frequently stumbled on stones and fell down hillsides. Yet they all recalled the words of the Israeli officers who told them, "Each one of you is going to carry on your back enough food to keep a hundred Jews alive another day." The "Burma Road" was completed a few days before the first truce began.

On June 11, 1948, the Jews and Arabs laid down their arms for a month-long truce. As one Israeli officer commented, the truce fell on the exhausted armies like "dew from heaven." Israel had suffered heavy casualties and had stretched its supplies to the breaking point. Although the existence of the Israeli state no longer seemed in doubt, fully one third of the territory allocated to Israel under the partition now lay in Arab hands. Galilee and Jerusalem were still threatened and the army was woefully undermanned and ill equipped.

During the truce, neither side was supposed to introduce new troops or weapons, and Jerusalem was allowed only enough food and water to last a month. But Ben-Gurion had absolutely no intention of abiding by these conditions. To do so, he thought,

Menachem Begin, head of the Jewish terrorist group *Irgun*, caused friction in the Israeli camp during the June 1948 cease-fire by resisting Ben-Gurion's attempt to unify several Jewish militias into the Israeli Defense Force (IDF). In 1977 Begin became prime minister.

would be suicidal. Instead, he ordered convoys of food and medicines rushed to Jerusalem. The underground Haganah armament factories turned out weapons at full speed. Tons of ammunition, artillery, planes, and tanks were secretly unloaded at deserted coastal sites. Jewish volunteer fighters from countries all over the world flocked to Israel. New soldiers included a Dutch millionaire, a Red Army veteran, and a Brooklyn policeman. By the end of the truce, Israeli forces had grown from 70,000 to 100,000 and were now equipped with heavy weaponry. For their part, the Arabs had taken little advantage of the truce.

The only serious problem the Israelis faced during the truce was internal dissension. On June 1, 1948,

Menachem Begin agreed to Ben-Gurion's request to integrate Irgun forces into the Israeli army. But tensions soon developed between the terrorist organization and the Israeli state. The Irgun had chartered an old navy vessel, the *Altalena*, to bring 1,000 immigrants along with a large cache of weapons into Israel. Begin insisted that 20 percent of the arms on board the *Altalena* be given to Irgun forces in Jerusalem. But Ben-Gurion had forbidden the Irgun to maintain a separate arsenal.

When the *Altalena* cast anchor off the coast, hundreds of Irgun supporters rushed to the beach to help unload the ship. Ben-Gurion ordered Israeli army units to surround the area and issued an ultimatum to Begin: either turn over the arms to the government or be attacked. Begin refused and the Israeli troops and Irgun forces battled throughout the night. Under cover of darkness, the *Altalena* slipped out to sea and raced toward Tel Aviv.

When the ship neared Tel Aviv, Irgun sympathizers swamped the beach. The Israeli army cordoned off the area but rumors spread that the Irgun was planning a civil war. The Israeli cabinet was divided on what steps to take to stem the burgeoning conflict. Some were horrified that Jewish blood had been spilled by other Jews and urged negotiating with Begin. However, Ben-Gurion convinced the majority to accept a strong course of action. He ordered the army to shell the ship; after a direct hit, the *Altalena* exploded, killing 14 Irgun men on board. That night on the Irgun underground radio, Begin charged that Ben-Gurion, whom he called "the crazy dictator," had tried to murder him. Ben-Gurion never regretted his decision to shell the ship.

One day before the ceasefire was scheduled to end, Egyptian troops renewed their attacks on the southern front. The reinvigorated Israeli army repeatedly hurled back the Egyptian assaults and launched an offensive of its own. During the next 10 days, the Israeli army scored dramatic gains, capturing large chunks of territory in Galilee and around Jerusalem. Israel's victories stunned the Arabs and the outside world but the Jews paid a terrible price for

Swedish Count Folke Bernadotte served as UN mediator during both of the Arab-Israeli cease-fires in the summer of 1948. After proposing a peace plan that seemed to favor the Arabs, he was assassinated by Jewish terrorists in the streets of Jerusalem.

> *Notice had been given to the world that henceforth Israel would be a country in which law and order would prevail and in which responsible government would demand respect and obedience.*
> —ROBERT ST. JOHN
> British journalist, on the bombing of the *Altalena*

their triumphs. Each new offensive brought mounting casualties and Ben-Gurion wondered whether these deaths were ultimately worth the gain. One father who had lost his son sent Ben-Gurion a book with the dedication: "To David Ben-Gurion—at your orders he fought, and at your orders he fell; may your name be blessed." Such selflessness and support amazed Ben-Gurion and redoubled his commitment to achieving victory.

A second truce went into effect on July 18, 1948. Swedish Count Folke Bernadotte, the UN mediator who had also supervised the first truce, was again assigned to direct negotiations for a permanent peace. Bernadotte was now convinced that the original UN partition resolution had been a mistake. He now proposed a drastically revised peace plan: the Negev would be given to the Arabs in exchange for Israeli control over Galilee; immigration to the Jewish state would be limited after two years; all Arab refugees would be resettled in their homes; and Transjordan would be granted control over Jerusalem. Both the Israelis and Arabs rejected the plan outright. The Jews, Ben-Gurion argued, had not lost countless lives defending their independent state simply to return half of it and relinquish any future control over immigration. Bernadotte's second proposal was more evenhanded but before either side could react to the new plan, the UN mediator was assassinated in the streets of Jerusalem by Lehi extremists. Ben-Gurion subsequently arrested members of the Lehi and Irgun as well and ordered all dissident organizations to be dissolved.

Bernadotte's tragic death evoked great sympathy around the world. Both the United States and Great Britain endorsed his proposal and Ben-Gurion feared that Israel would be forced to grant substantial concessions in order to achieve peace. Israel's only alternative, he decided, was to go on the offensive: to take decisive military action that would present the Arabs and the world with a *fait accompli*. Ben-Gurion proposed launching a massive attack against the Egyptians to liberate the embattled Negev Desert. The only sticking point was to figure out how Israel could avoid being blamed for violating the ceasefire.

On October 14 an unarmed Israeli convoy crossing Egyptian lines under UN supervision suddenly exploded. Unknown to the UN observers, who naturally laid the blame on the Egyptians, the Israelis themselves had dynamited their own trucks. With a perfect pretext for ending the truce, the Israeli armies attacked with furious speed. By mid-December the Israeli troops had not only captured the entire Negev but were driving across Egypt's Sinai Peninsula in perfect position to invade the Gaza Strip and capture the Egyptian army. Ben-Gurion, however, desired peace more than territory. The Israeli troops withdrew from Egyptian soil and on

> *Bernadotte suffered the tragic destiny of many other good men who with the noblest of motives try to part two combatants.*
> —MAURICE EDELMAN
> British historian, on the UN official assigned to mediate the 1948–49 Arab-Israeli War

AP/WIDE WORLD

Arab families flee toward Lebanon from their homes in Galilee in November 1948. By the end of the war, Israel had not only repulsed the Arab invasion but also had significantly expanded its frontiers to include Jaffa, western Galilee, and the modern half ("New City") of Jerusalem.

January 7, 1949, hostilities ended. A few months later the Israelis reached armistice agreements with Egypt, Transjordan, Lebanon, and Syria.

Ben-Gurion's nation survived at a terrible cost. Six thousand Jews were killed during the war. The city of Jerusalem was divided in half: the Wailing Wall, the old Jewish quarter, the Temple Mount, and other religious monuments within Jerusalem's ancient walls would be closed to Israel for almost 20 years. Between 700,000 and 1 million Palestinian Arabs were now exiled to refugee camps in the surrounding Arab countries, a legacy of the bitter war.

In a famous novel by S. Yizhar, depicting Israel's War of Independence, the hero's last words poignantly capture the bittersweet feelings that Israelis felt in victory. "The hill is ours; the fields, the wide expanses, the country. Yet have we truly finished?" Ben-Gurion would try to answer this troubling question in the coming years.

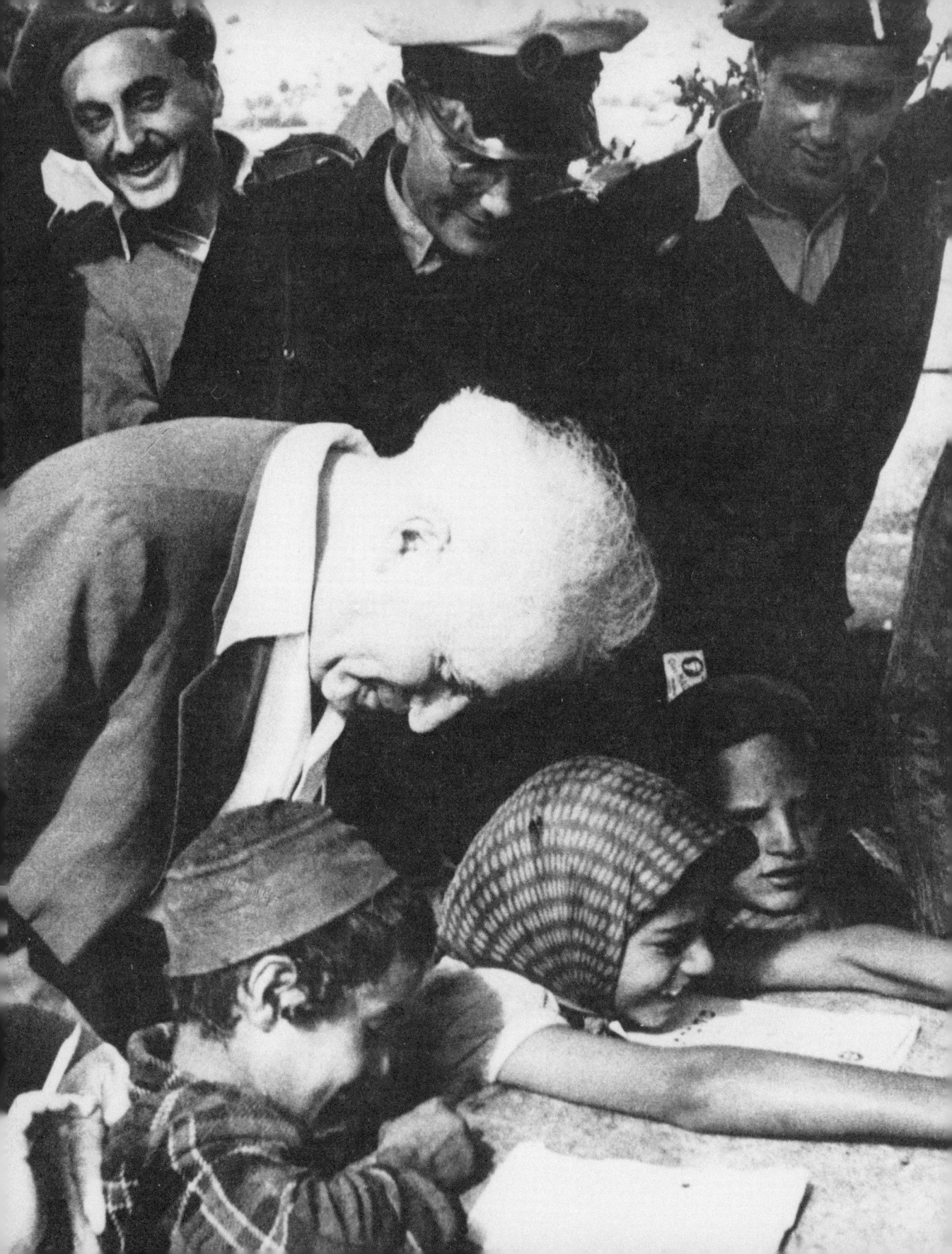

8
Prime Minister

Israel was devastated by the war: its economy was virtually bankrupt, its land had been destroyed, and its population had grown weary from the trials and tribulations of the past years. But Ben-Gurion, who became prime minister of Israel after the nation's first elections in March 1949, insisted that there was yet another mountain to climb. A Jewish state had always been envisioned as a shining beacon for all Jews around the world; the time had come for this dream to be fulfilled. Jews exiled from their ancestral homeland, Ben-Gurion argued, should be urged to return without any limitation or exception. Prominent members of the cabinet and Ben-Gurion's own party were aghast at his suggestion. They worried that unrestricted immigration would bring about the collapse of the fragile state. A nation of only 700,000 people could not possibly hope to absorb hundreds of thousands of immigrants each year; they argued instead for a gradual immigration program.

Ben-Gurion dismissed such warnings. An expanded population, he argued, would help to enlarge the army, to reclaim the country's vast open spaces, and to create a modernized economy. Furthermore, unlimited immigration would enable

Few men in history have had to face so many problems, such intensity of opposition, such diverse discouragement.
—ROBERT ST. JOHN
British journalist, on
Ben-Gurion as prime minister

In the 1950s, Prime Minister Ben-Gurion talks playfully with children at a camp for recent immigrants to Israel. At Ben-Gurion's urging, the *Knesset*, the Israeli parliament, passed the "Law of Return" in 1950, allowing any Jew in the world the right to immigrate to Israel.
DAVID BEN-GURION CENTENNIAL COMMISSION

In 1950 in a program called the "Magic Carpet," Israel airlifted thousands of Jews out of Yemen, where they had been a repressed minority. In this picture, Yemeni immigrants wait patiently for instructions underneath the outdated jet that brought them to the promised land.

Jews in Arab countries, whose lives had been threatened since the War of Independence, to escape oppression. For these Jews, known as *Sephardic* (or oriental), immigration had become essential for survival. All these factors persuaded Ben-Gurion to risk uncontrolled mass immigration. Ben-Gurion single-handedly browbeat the Mapai and the cabinet into accepting the "Law of Return," which granted the right to any Jew to immigrate to Israel. It would prove to be his most significant decision as prime minister.

Between May 15, 1948, and June 30, 1953, the Jewish population in Israel doubled. Between May 14 and December 31, 1948, more than 100,000 immigrants arrived; in 1949, 239,576; in 1950, 170,249. Within five years almost 700,000 new immigrants had entered the country. On many occasions, the immigrants reached Israel because of marvelously ingenious and improvised plans. Operation "Magic Carpet," for instance, was hastily organized to airlift Jews out the Arab country of Yemen. Israel purchased several outdated airplanes and began a regular shuttle service, seven flights each day, until all the Yemeni Jews were resettled. Similar schemes brought Jews from Egypt, Iraq, Syria, Morocco, and Eastern Europe. Ben-Gurion later wrote that these first memorable years of Israel were "the greatest years in Jewish history since the Maccabean victory over the Greeks, 2,113 years before the rebirth of the state in our times."

Despite Ben-Gurion's optimism, Israel proved ill equipped to handle this tidal wave of refugees. Many immigrants had to be housed in abandoned Arab villages and neighborhoods or in cheap prefabricated homes constructed by the government. Yet neither were adequate and eventually the most realistic solution became massive tent cities. Immigrants were settled in tattered canvas structures that offered little protection from the heavy rains and chill of winter or the miserable heat of summer. By 1951, 17,000 tents in 53 camps were home to 97,000 men, women, and children — almost one tenth of Israel's entire population. Life in the camps was a grim ordeal: diseases, such as tuberculosis

Between 1948 and 1953, more than 700,000 Jews immigrated to Israel, doubling the nation's population. Because Israel did not have nearly enough housing to absorb such a massive influx, thousands of new settlers were forced to live in enormous tent cities, where conditions were often primitive. At many camps, immigrant families had to bathe and wash their laundry at communal wells (inset).

UPI/BETTMANN NEWSPHOTOS

> *Israel must accomplish in a few years what has taken others generations.*
> —DAVID BEN-GURION

and malaria, were rampant; there were no jobs for adults and precious few schools for the children.

In 1949 Ben-Gurion presided over the reorganization of Israel's political structure. Under the nation's proportional election system, citizens cast ballots for parties rather than individual candidates. For instance, if a party received 50 percent of the vote, it was entitled to 60 seats in the 120-seat *Knesset* (legislative assembly). Then the first 60 people in the party's list, ranked in order of importance, took seats in the Knesset. (Ben-Gurion, of course, was ranked first on the Mapai list.) Each government had to operate with narrow legislative majorities; this created a built-in incentive for political blackmail by the smaller parties over the larger ones.

Although the Mapai was Israel's governing party for almost 30 years, it never enjoyed a plurality of more than 39.2 percent. After each election, Ben-Gurion remained prime minister on the basis of a narrow coalition. This typically entailed accepting a partnership with the small religious parties and subsequently compromising the Mapai's original policies and principles. Ben-Gurion wanted a free hand to decide foreign policy and national political issues; in return the religious leaders were given a free hand over religious issues. This eventually led to a prohibition of civil marriages or divorce, government support for religious schools, and implementation of Sabbath laws, whereby shops, offices, theaters, and public transportation were closed on

David and Paula Ben-Gurion cast their votes in Israel's first election on January 29, 1949. The election gave the Mapai party control of the Knesset, which it would dominate for the next 30 years. Under Israel's new parliamentary system, the majority party's leader, Ben-Gurion, automatically became prime minister.

the Sabbath (sundown Friday evening through sundown Saturday evening). Conservative religious leaders were ultimately granted control over many important areas of private conscience, an anathema to Ben-Gurion's colleagues in the Mapai, who charged he had betrayed the original secular goals of the party. The ever pragmatic Ben-Gurion, however, argued that a safe and secure nation was well worth the price of some "insignificant" concessions.

Israel's security continued to be a paramount concern of Ben-Gurion. Of course this was partly dictated by Israel's unique geographical predicament — a true strategist's nightmare. Israel had more than 600 miles of frontiers, and no village or settlement was located more than 18 miles from an Arab border. Eilat, Israel's Red Sea gateway to Asia and Africa on the Gulf of Aqaba, was extremely susceptible to a naval blockade.

This vulnerability was exacerbated by the hardening of Arab policy toward Israel in the early 1950s. In 1949 Israel proposed, without success, to readmit to the country and resettle as many as 100,000 Palestinian Arab refugees in return for a peace agreement with her Arab neighbors. But this offer came at a time when, for Arab leaders, it was politically dangerous to discuss making peace with Israel. Earlier in 1949, Egyptian Minister of Finance Amin Osmon Pasha had been assassinated by the fanatical Muslim Brotherhood merely for accepting a ceasefire agreement. Later, on July 30, 1951, King Abdullah of Jordan, who had made several overtures to Israel, was assassinated by a gunman hired by Arabs who opposed negotiating with Israel. Even many Arabs who were moderate before 1948 expressed bitter hatred for the Jews after 1948.

Ben-Gurion's foreign policy was appropriately pragmatic and tough-minded. He viewed Israel's position vis-à-vis the Arabs as analogous to the legend of David and Goliath. Israel was bound to be the perpetual David. For all its military accomplishments, Israel's security would always depend on establishing an alliance with a large power. Israel at first hoped Great Britain could play that role: Ben-Gurion even suggested that Great Britain be allowed

Abdullah, who became king of Transjordan in 1946 (Jordan after 1949) when his country attained its independence, holds an outdoor conference in the courtyard of Raghadan Palace. After attempting to negotiate peace with Israel, Abdullah was assassinated by a Palestinian nationalist in 1951, accelerating a downward spiral in Arab-Israeli relations.

> *We shall suffer any torture they think up for us to prevent a decision to deal with Germany!*
>
> —MENACHEM BEGIN
> opposition leader, 1952

Ben-Gurion and Abba Eban (center), Israel's ambassador to the UN, present U.S. president Harry S. Truman with a *menorah* (a candelabra used in Jewish worship) on his birthday in 1951. After recognizing Israel's right to exist in 1949, the United States gradually became its most important ally.

to establish air and naval bases in the country in return for providing Israel with military aid. Yet, Britain's lingering ties to the Arab world precluded any long-term arrangement.

Over time, the United States became Israel's primary military ally. Ben-Gurion had always seen Israel as a bastion of the West in the Middle East: an alliance with the United States, Ben-Gurion said, would be a "partnership linked to human freedom and to a democratic system of government." Yet, Ben-Gurion realized even if Israel developed a warm relationship with the United States, their alliance would always be contingent and conditional. "Let us not fool ourselves into thinking that America ever identified with or will ever identify in the future with the state of Israel," Ben-Gurion warned. "America has never committed itself, nor will it ever do so, to stand behind us in all of what we shall do or want."

The most controversial foreign policy issue in the first years of the Israeli state involved relations with Germany. In March 1951 Israeli representatives held secret talks with Konrad Adenauer, the chancellor of the recently formed German Federal Republic (West Germany). The German leader agreed to pay reparations to Israel for Jewish property destroyed by the Nazis. The reparations were in no way intended as compensation for the millions of Jews who had lost their lives but were to be regarded as financial aid to enable Israel to absorb the hundreds of thousands of Holocaust survivors. Ben-Gurion felt the justification for reparations "lay in the final injunction of the inarticulate six million. The victims of Nazism, whose very murder was a ringing cry for Israel to rise, to be strong and prosperous, to safeguard her peace and security, and so prevent such a disaster from ever again overwhelming the Jewish people."

The acceptance of reparations elicited widespread protests throughout Israel. Members of Ben-Gurion's own party opposed accepting what they called "unholy" money from a nation they considered to be murderers. Menachem Begin attacked reparations as the "ultimate abomination" and threatened a campaign of violent resistance if reparations were

AP/WIDE WORLD

agreed to. In a mass demonstration outside the Knesset, Begin charged that the issue was a "battle of life and death." Protesters pushed their way through the police cordon, set fire to automobiles, and threw rocks and bricks at the Knesset buildings. Ben-Gurion admitted in a Knesset debate that no compensation was "restitution for the loss of human life or expiation for sufferings and agonies of men and women, children, old people and infants." However, Ben-Gurion questioned why the German people should continue to be the beneficiaries of the murder and plunder of Jews. Ben-Gurion's vigorous leadership and eloquence carried the day; on January 9, 1952, the Knesset voted by 61 to 50 to accept reparations. In February Israel signed an agreement whereby West Germany would provide $715 million in goods to Israel and would also contribute $107 million to world Jewish organizations.

Israeli police flood a Jerusalem street with blazing streams of gasoline, attempting to disperse crowds of demonstrators who stormed the Knesset in early 1952. The riots protested the Israeli government's decision to accept $822 million from the West German government in reparation for Hitler's atrocities against the Jews.

9
A Famous Kibbutznik

Ben-Gurion was returning from a trip to Eilat at the southern tip of Israel in May 1953, when he encountered a group of young people hard at work in the heart of the Negev desert. They told Ben-Gurion that they had fought in that area during the War of Independence and later had returned to establish a kibbutz named Sdeh Boker. One of the kibbutzniks jokingly suggested to Ben-Gurion that he retire and move to their settlement. Upon reflection, Ben-Gurion was surprised to find how much this seemingly absurd idea appealed to him. The "Old Man," now 67 years old, was emotionally exhausted from five years of constant challenges and crises. Perhaps it was time to return to the pioneering life he had forsaken so many years before.

A stay in Sdeh Boker held the promise of a much needed respite from the travails of leadership and, paradoxically, of improving his political career. Ben-Gurion's temporary absence from the political arena might demonstrate once and for all how valuable his leadership was. In 1953 Ben-Gurion resigned

> *I am not a member of the government any more. I am just a member of the Knesset who is working in a stable.*
> —DAVID BEN-GURION
> speaking in 1954,
> after resigning the
> prime ministership

In December 1953 Ben-Gurion shocked his country by resigning as prime minister and moving to Sdeh Boker, a remote *kibbutz*, or agricultural settlement, in the Negev desert. Here, the founder of Israel does manual labor at the kibbutz, feeding a young sheep from a baby bottle.
UPI/BETTMANN NEWSPHOTOS

> *His belief in Israel's future required him personally to go into the desert with his wife, and so by his example give a leadership which exhortation alone could not possibly offer.*
> —MAURICE EDELMAN
> British historian, on Ben-Gurion's retirement to Sdeh Boker

from power. His country was shocked. Few leaders of his stature and authority have ever voluntarily stepped down from power. Ben-Gurion broadcast an inspired farewell, quoting from the Book of Psalms, "Lord, my heart is not haughty, nor mine eyes lofty; neither do I exercise myself in great matters, or in things too high for me."

Ben-Gurion and Paula arrived in Sdeh Boker in December 1953 to begin their new life. Ben-Gurion wrote to a friend, "I feel as I did in my first days in the land." Indeed, Ben-Gurion's first task in the kibbutz was hauling manure, precisely what he had done on his first day in Petach Tikvah 47 years earlier. Determined to prove himself worthy of membership, Ben-Gurion insisted that members of the kibbutz call him David and threw himself into difficult manual work. As a concession to his advanced years, the kibbutz soon relieved Ben-Gurion from fieldwork and placed him in charge of feeding the kibbutz's newborn lambs. Ben-Gurion was happy and content. He slept much easier and, after a few months, his health improved considerably. The time in Sdeh Boker also bettered his relationship with Paula. The kibbutz built Ben-Gurion and Paula a one-story, four-room prefabricated house with a screened porch. It was a comfortable house,

American journalist Edward R. Murrow interviews the famous kibbutznik David Ben-Gurion for the CBS television show "See It Now." They are seated on a patio in front of Ben-Gurion's four-room house at Sdeh Boker kibbutz.

UPI/BETTMANN NEWSPHOTOS

Moshe Sharett, who took over as Israeli prime minister following Ben-Gurion's retirement in 1953, meets with the "Old Man" at Sdeh Boker in 1955. During the visit, Sharett convinced his predecessor to leave his peaceful life in the Negev and to return to the Israeli government as defense minister.

equipped with modern conveniences. Its focus was Ben-Gurion's study, which was crammed with more than 5,000 books.

Ben-Gurion's idyll in the Negev was to be short-lived, however. During his absence, sharp conflicts had developed among members of his successor's cabinet. The new prime minister, Moshe Sharett, was a brilliant man but lacked Ben-Gurion's leadership skills or charisma. His defense minister, Pinhas Lavon, an egotistical man, treated him with open contempt, refusing to consult with him on important military issues. Lavon also had attacked two of Ben-Gurion's young protégés: Shimon Peres, who was director general of the ministry of defense, and Moshe Dayan, the army chief of staff.

These rivalries played a major role in the Lavon affair of 1954. The history of the scandal begins with the ascension to power in Egypt of General Gamal Abdel Nasser. Worried that Nasser's radical Arab nationalism might pose a threat to Israel's security, Israel's Intelligence Chief Benjamin Gibly hatched a wild scheme to discredit the Egyptian's regime. A group of Israeli spies would bomb Western embassies and offices in Egypt and blame the acts on the Muslim Brotherhood. The sabotage would prove to the world that Nasser's regime was unstable and incapable of maintaining order. Defense Minister Lavon supported the plan and in late May, Gibly gave the go-ahead to his agents in Egypt. The plan was horribly botched, however, and the Israeli agents were arrested in July.

After Egypt began a well-publicized trial of the agents in December (two were eventually executed for treason), an Israeli commission of inquiry was formed to investigate responsibility for the dangerous plan. The Lavon investigation was the most closely guarded secret in Israel; even cabinet ministers and Knesset members were kept in the dark. Both Gibly and Lavon disclaimed responsibility for the fiasco but a later investigation found that both men had committed perjury to avoid being implicated in the matter. Although the commission of inquiry was unable to reach a conclusive verdict, Lavon was quietly pressured into resigning his post to avoid any publicity about the incident.

Ben-Gurion's colleagues in the Mapai convinced him to take over the position as defense minister. As one of his first acts, three weeks after his appointment, Ben-Gurion approved a reprisal raid into Egypt in retaliation for the murder of a Jewish man by Egyptian intelligence agents. One hundred and fifty paratroopers attacked an Egyptian army base near the Gaza Strip. Eight Israelis were killed; thirty-eight Egyptians died and thirty more were wounded. There was again considerable disagreement between Ben-Gurion and Sharett about the

As Israeli defense minister, Ben-Gurion maintained a hard-line policy toward the Arabs, approving several limited strikes against neighboring countries in retaliation for Arab guerrilla activity. The Israeli raids contributed to an escalating cycle of terror and revenge.

Gamal Abdel Nasser (foreground), a charismatic military officer who became president of Egypt after overthrowing King Farouk in 1952. Nasser's unique fusion of socialist economic principles and an aggressively independent foreign policy captivated his countrymen but caused worry in Western governments.

propriety of the raid. In many respects Sharett's reservations were well founded, for the reprisal policy was neither farsighted nor especially effective. Israeli retaliatory attacks only increased the defiance of the Egyptian government and the murderousness of the guerrilla raids.

After the Gaza raid, Nasser set up *Fedayeen* (suicide units) to launch attacks on Israel. In September Nasser announced a new arms deal with the Soviet bloc; the quantities promised were enormous, and the Israelis feared that the military balance between the two countries might now be destroyed.

Ben-Gurion was appointed prime minister again in November 1955, with Moshe Sharett serving as foreign minister. The atmosphere was tense and warlike. A month earlier, Egypt had blockaded the Strait of Tiran, thereby effectively closing off Israel's navigation to Asia and Africa. Ben-Gurion instructed Moshe Dayan, army chief of staff, to prepare war plans for three different contingencies: an occupation of the Gaza Strip, an offensive into the northern Sinai, and the capture of the Strait of Tiran to crush the Egyptian blockade.

Ben-Gurion asked the United States for a substantial arms agreement in order to offset the Soviet aid to Egypt. President Dwight D. Eisenhower, determined to avoid a confrontation with the Soviet Union, refused the Israeli request. Instead, Eisen-

> *Israel can win a hundred battles yet its problem will not be solved; but if the Arabs are victorious only once, it will mean our end.*
> —DAVID BEN-GURION

hower sent a diplomatic envoy, Robert Anderson, to meet with both Ben-Gurion and Nasser in the hopes of reaching a peaceful compromise. Nasser, in exchange for peace, demanded that Israel allow the Arab refugees a choice between returning to their homes in Israel or receiving compensation for their property. Ben-Gurion refused to compromise on the question of refugees: "I think that one should prevent their return," he argued. "War is war and those who declared war upon us will have to bear the consequences after they have been defeated."

Ben-Gurion, however, proposed a personal meeting with the Egyptian leader; he believed that only a face-to-face confrontation could lead to a meaningful settlement. Nasser refused to meet with Ben-Gurion, perhaps wary that a public encounter with the Israeli leader would be an unpopular policy move in Egypt. With the failure of the envoy's mission, the United States refused Israel's second request for weapons. An angry Ben-Gurion warned that if the United States did not assist Israel, "then we shall have one single duty: to safeguard our security. Nothing else will engage our attention."

Nasser announced his plan to nationalize the Suez Canal on July 26, 1956. Representatives from Israel, France, and Great Britain met secretly to discuss ways of overthrowing Nasser. Both great powers had their own motivations for wanting to eliminate the Egyptian leader. France, bogged down in a bloody colonial war in Algeria, wanted to remove Nasser because of his support for the Algerian rebels. The British hoped to recapture their lost influence in the Middle East. Ben-Gurion wrote, "This is a unique opportunity [in that] two powers will try to eliminate Nasser and we will not face him alone as he grows stronger."

A secret treaty was reached between the three governments on October 23. Israel would attack Egypt and occupy most of the Sinai. France and England would immediately call for a ceasefire and they would then use the attack as a pretext for taking up positions on either side of the Suez Canal, under the pretense of protecting the canal against the two warring sides. France would provide air cover and

> *The British government, which sold the Egyptian dictator heavy tanks knowing they were intended to strike at Israel, obstinately refused to sell them to Israel.*
>
> —DAVID BEN-GURION
> on the balance of power in the Middle East

logistical support to Israel to prevent the Egyptians from bombing Israeli territory.

Israeli troops launched their attack against Egypt on October 29, 1956. Although the opposing forces were roughly equivalent, Israel's imaginative and daring campaign produced spectacular results. At the cost of only 180 men killed and 4 captured, Israel was able to occupy the entire Sinai Peninsula and Gaza Strip in only 8 days; they destroyed 3 Egyptian army divisions, killed 2,000 soldiers and captured 6,000 prisoners. Ben-Gurion, in a speech before the Knesset, intimated that Israel planned to annex the entire Sinai Peninsula.

When Nasser rejected the Anglo-French ceasefire ultimatum, British and French troops commenced their own operations in Egypt on November 5. That same day however, the Soviet Union sent a sharp note to France, England, and Israel, warning them to halt their aggression or else risk possible Soviet intervention. President Eisenhower, likewise, began to exert tremendous pressure on his two Eu-

The Ras Tanura oil refinery in Saudi Arabia. British leaders determined that Nasser's nationalization of the Suez Canal threatened Western access to Middle Eastern oil and secretly agreed with France and Israel to invade Egypt in 1956.

Thousands of angry Israelis gather in downtown Jerusalem in March 1957 to protest Ben-Gurion's withdrawal of Israeli troops from the Sinai Peninsula, which had been captured from Egypt in the 1956 campaign. The Israeli withdrawal came in response to intense pressure from the UN.

ropean allies. The UN General Assembly voted overwhelmingly to order Israel to withdraw unconditionally from the Sinai. For a few days, the world held its breath while a nuclear war appeared to be a distinct possibility. Eventually, Great Britain and France capitulated under the pressure and withdrew their troops from Egypt.

Ben-Gurion, in a rare admission of error, confessed that he had probably gone too far in his Knesset speech: "I was too drunk with victory." Israel began to withdraw from the Sinai in installments, quickly enough to avoid a political showdown with the United States but slowly enough perhaps to enable them to keep some territory. Eisenhower threatened in 1957 that any further procrastination would lead to a break in United States–Israeli relations. Finally, in late January, Israel withdrew all of its troops to the same 1949 borders with which it began the war.

In the short run, Ben-Gurion's military victory resulted in a political defeat. Nasser emerged from the military debacle with his political prestige intact; indeed, he quickly became one of the most popular leaders in the Third World for his underdog fight against the Western powers. No new territory had been achieved and the guerrilla threats to Israeli frontier settlements still existed. Yet, in the long run, Israel's security was greatly enhanced, for the Sinai campaign brought Israel 10 years of peace. The war dramatically improved the morale of the Israeli population; the Israelis' future feelings of military invincibility were certainly rooted in their overwhelming military victory. Israel also learned a valuable lesson about the advantages of a preemptive attack; knowledge they would put to use in just a little more than a decade.

10
And the Deserts Will Bloom

> *We will make the wasteland fruitful and turn it into a garden of Eden.*
> —DAVID BEN-GURION

Ben-Gurion reached his seventies as one of the world's most respected leaders. The "Old Man" had guided his small, fledgling nation to epic achievements. Arid desert had been transformed into fertile farmland, and thriving cities had been created out of uninhabited swamplands. A strong military, a modern economy, and a lively democracy had been built in just over a decade. Israel had established strong ties with many of the emerging African nations, and with Iran and Turkey in the Middle East. And, in 1960, Ben-Gurion exchanged an historic handshake with the prime minister of West Germany, Konrad Adenauer, leading to the establishment of formal diplomatic relations between the two nations, at last officially reconciling the Jewish people with their former German adversaries.

Ben-Gurion's prestige and popularity reached its peak in May 1960, when he announced to a stunned Knesset that Israel had captured the notorious Nazi war criminal Adolf Eichmann in Argentina and would be placing him on trial. Ben-Gurion believed the trial of Eichmann would remind both the world and his own people why a Jewish state was so vitally important. "For the first time in Jewish history,

A formal portrait of Ben-Gurion toward the end of his political career. Respected as one of the greatest statesmen of his time, the "Old Man" had guided tiny Israel from a fledgling nation to a productive democracy.

UPI/BETTMANN NEWSPHOTOS

In 1960 Adolf Eichmann, a former officer in the Nazi secret police, was captured by Israeli agents and then put on trial in Jerusalem for his crimes against Jews during World War II. In this picture, Eichmann listens in a bullet-proof booth as a judge (not visible) sentences him to death.

historical justice is being done by the sovereign Jewish people," Ben-Gurion declared. "For many generations it was we who suffered, who were tortured, were killed, and were judged. For the first time, Israel is judging the murderers of the Jewish people." Eichmann was convicted of his war crimes and executed.

Ben-Gurion was lucky to be alive to enjoy the historic moment. On October 29, 1957, he had been sitting behind his desk in the middle of the Knesset chamber, when a young man in the top row of the crowded gallery suddenly stood up and threw a small grenade, which dropped just a few feet from him. Seconds later, a deafening explosion rocked the walls of the parliament. A cabinet minister who had been sitting several rows behind Ben-Gurion fell to the floor with blood pouring from his head and stomach. Ben-Gurion was hit by splinters in his arms and legs but was not seriously injured. The bombing was the work of a young man with a history of mental illness, seeking to avenge some imaginary wrong by a government agency. Ben-Gurion wrote a letter to the parents of the young man: "I know that you regret, as do all the people of Israel, the abominable and senseless crime that your son committed yesterday. You are not to blame. You are living in Israel where justice reigns, and I wish you and your son good luck. May you succeed in educating the rest of your children to do good deeds and to love Israel."

Ben-Gurion's brush with death was a strong reminder of his own mortality. Perhaps the time had come for his party to bring new blood into the leadership. Ben-Gurion recommended to his colleagues at a Mapai party conference in 1958 that a new generation must now join the veterans in the leadership of the party and the state. Since the early 1950s, Ben-Gurion had carefully promoted a number of young disciples to key government positions. Among them were such brilliant young men as Moshe Dayan, Shimon Peres, Abba Eban (later Israeli ambassador to the UN) and Teddy Kollek (later mayor of Jerusalem).

Many of the older Mapai veterans were suspicious of the ambitious and arrogant young technocrats. They felt Ben-Gurion's disciples had little attachment to the original social ideas and principles of the party. Dayan, for instance, had criticized the outmoded beliefs of the kibbutzniks and men of the Histadrut. "The men of the last generation have reached an age where they can no longer carry out revolutions." Dayan complained further, "These men look back proudly on their achievements of 1902 . . . but we are interested in 1962."

But Ben-Gurion's faith in his young protégés remained strong. He made sure they were placed on Mapai's Knesset slate in the 1959 elections, and he used his own popularity to promote their electoral campaigns. The November 1959 elections turned out to be the Mapai's greatest political triumph. The stunning victory was attributed to the invigorating presence of the younger candidates on the list. Nonetheless, the election results did little to heal dissension within the Mapai. A coalition of veterans (Moshe Sharett, Golda Meir, and Pinhas Lavon, who had been restored to the party's top leadership) joined forces to oppose Ben-Gurion and his protégés. This generational conflict would decisively affect the convulsive political events of the early 1960s.

In 1957 an Israeli intelligence agent was arrested on suspicion of being a double agent for Egypt. This same agent had been intimately involved in 1954 in the Lavon affair. Now the spy revealed that during this earlier scandal, he had committed perjury and forgery under instructions from Israel's intelligence chief who had hoped to implicate Defense Minister Lavon in the incident. Lavon demanded that Ben-Gurion completely exonerate him from any wrongdoing in the affair. Ben-Gurion insisted on remaining an impartial observer; a ministerial committee was therefore formed in 1960 to investigate Lavon's claims. The committee did not follow strict judicial rules of procedure and quickly disintegrated into a political forum. Reports of testimony before the committee were leaked to Israel's newspapers, and

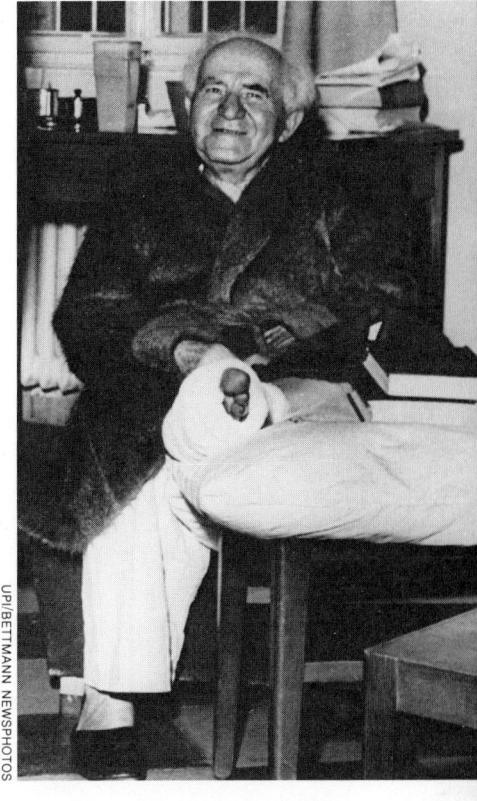

His injured leg propped on a pillow, Ben-Gurion smiles for photographers in his hospital room. Along with several other Israeli politicians, the prime minister was wounded in October 1957 when an Israeli with a history of mental problems threw a grenade in the Knesset chamber.

> *We must teach the youth what happened.*
> —DAVID BEN-GURION
> on the capture and trial of Adolf Eichmann in 1960

although the censor's restrictions forced the papers to couch the testimony in code names, everyone in Israel soon was aware that the government was in the midst of a major scandal.

The committee ruled on December 20, 1960, that Lavon was not to blame for the Egyptian debacle. But Ben-Gurion refused to accept the committee's recommendations and launched a vicious personal attack on Lavon, whom he suspected of leaking testimony to the press. In January 1961 he threatened to resign. Mapai leaders, he insisted, must choose between him and Lavon. They chose to dismiss Lavon. But the affair created bitter resentment. Many saw Ben-Gurion's attacks on Lavon as motivated by personal rather than public concerns. The "Old Man," his critics argued, had urged a fair, impartial hearing yet rejected the findings because of his own petty vindictiveness. The Lavon affair undermined Ben-Gurion's credibility among the Israeli populace and led to a permanent break between Ben-Gurion and many of his Mapai comrades. Ben-Gurion would head the Israeli government for another 20 months, but his power would never be quite the same.

After a year and a half of turmoil, Ben-Gurion resigned as prime minister on June 15, 1963. For the first time his Mapai colleagues did not beg him to stay on. Ben-Gurion's protégés were removed from their positions, as the veterans quickly reasserted their control of the party. Even after he stepped down, Ben-Gurion continued to attack his Mapai comrades for their handling of the Lavon affair. At a party conference in 1965, some of Ben-Gurion's veteran comrades bitterly attacked his character. Golda Meir called him a hypocrite who "speaks of justice but accuses and judges from the outset."

In the face of his comrades' attacks, Ben-Gurion split from the Mapai and formed his own party, the *Rafi*. The 1965 campaign was the longest, dirtiest campaign in Israel's history, marked by sickening insults and countercharges among the former friends. In the election, the Labor Alignment (Mapai's coalition with other labor parties) won 45

> *It is true that the Lord did not put soil on all the rocks, but that was only because He wanted us to have the satisfaction of putting it there ourselves.*
> —DAVID BEN-GURION

seats, the Rafi only 10. The results were enough to relegate Ben-Gurion to political oblivion; as one commentator noted, the campaign seemed to be "a referendum on whether the Old Man was really an old man."

On May 15, 1967, large battalions of the Egyptian army moved across the Suez Canal and took up positions in the Sinai near the Israeli border. Nasser stated, "Our basic objective will be to destroy Israel." Israel partially mobilized its reserves but people openly questioned whether new Prime Minister Levi Eshkol was a fit leader for wartime. The public clamored for Ben-Gurion to be placed at the head of a government of national unity. But Ben-Gurion responded by outspokenly opposing military action against Egypt. His supporters reluctantly concluded that the "Old Man" was no longer the audacious leader that they remembered. Charles de Gaulle commented: "He is living in a world that passed him by."

During the 1967 Six-Day War, Israeli soldiers (inset) occupied the Old City of Jerusalem, giving Israel, for the first time in its history, control of the Wailing Wall. A sacred site that attracts Jews from around the world for private sessions of prayer, the wall is the only piece left standing of the Second Temple, which was built by the Jews in the 6th century B.C.

> *I very much doubt that the Jewish people will ever produce a greater leader or a more astute and courageous statesman.*
>
> —GOLDA MEIR
> Israeli prime minister,
> 1969 to 1974,
> on Ben-Gurion

David and Paula Ben-Gurion stand in the doorway of their Sdeh Boker home, to which they returned after his retirement from politics in 1967. In his final years Ben-Gurion divided his time between daily manual labor and writing.

The Six-Day War, which erupted on June 5, 1967, was a watershed event, a milestone for both Israel and Ben-Gurion. It had an enormous impact on international relations in the Middle East. Israel won a crushing military victory, in which its national territory was almost doubled. It had captured the Sinai Peninsula and the Gaza Strip from Egypt, the Golan Heights from Syria, and the West bank of the Jordan River from Jordan. And, for the first time in more than 2,000 years, all of Jerusalem again belonged to the Jews. Israel's new domains, referred to as "occupied territories," expanded the nation's Arab population to more than 1 million, a fact that would affect Israeli politics and society for years to come. The Six-Day War also marked the true end of the Ben-Gurion era. Before the fighting began, many had looked to the "Old Man" as the only one capable of saving the nation; by its conclusion, Ben-Gurion was seen as a retired leader whose time had passed.

Ben-Gurion spent his remaining years in quiet retirement at Sdeh Boker. He devoted himself to writing his memoirs and a history of Israel. The bitter squabbles that brought Ben-Gurion's career to an end would soon seem trivial. Memories of those events would be replaced in the national consciousness by the image of Ben-Gurion as "the Father of his Nation." His 85th birthday was declared a national holiday by the government. No longer a man of war, Ben-Gurion now reexamined many of his former precepts. The "Old Man" shocked many visitors by advocating Israeli withdrawal from all the occupied territories except Jerusalem. How could Israel rule 1 million Arabs, he asked, and still remain a healthy democracy? Ben-Gurion feared that peace might prove to be a distant, elusive goal for the Jewish nation. He wrote to his old friend Rachel Bet-Halachmi (née Nelkin), whose friendship he had rekindled in his last decade: "There is hope dear Rachel, that peace is approaching, not quickly, but slowly, slowly and it appears to me that by the end of this century, the prophecy of Isaiah will be fulfilled."

Ben-Gurion reads intently in his library at Sdeh Boker. The man who devoted his life to establishing a Jewish state in Palestine died on December 1, 1973.

Paula died in 1968. In all their years of marriage, Paula had never fully shared Ben-Gurion's dreams, but she remained with him — through the hardships as well as the triumphs. Ben-Gurion wrote afterward, "Paula was unique. She was a friend, a wife, a mother, a child, a sister — she was Paula." Paula's death deeply affected Ben-Gurion; without the burden of politics he finally realized how much he missed her. "After Paula died," said her closest friend, "Ben-Gurion was more sentimental and human. No one believed he would grieve so much. No one thought he was capable of it."

Ben-Gurion's health collapsed a few days before the Yom Kippur War erupted in October 1973. The "Old Man" was struck by a cerebral hemorrhage that left him paralyzed and speechless; for a while he remained fully conscious and his piercing eyes were still alive to every visitor. It was truly an irony of history that both Ben-Gurion and the state he created would be fighting for survival at the same time. Ben-Gurion died on December 1, 1973, and was buried by his wife's side near Sdeh Boker. Their graves overlook the timeless landscape of the Negev desert, site of the Jews' first struggle for freedom: it was a fitting tribute for the man whom many called "the greatest Jew in more than 2,000 years."

Further Reading

Bar-Zohar. Michael. *Ben-Gurion: A Biography.* New York: Delacorte, 1978.

Ben-Gurion, David. *Israel: A Personal History.* New York: Sabra, 1972.

Dayan, Moshe. *Diary of the Sinai Campaign.* Westport, Connecticut: Greenwood Press, 1979.

Edelman, Maurice. *David: The Story of Ben-Gurion.* New York: Putnam, 1965.

Kurzman, Dan. *Prophet of Fire: Ben-Gurion of Israel.* New York: Simon & Schuster, 1983.

McAuley, Karen. *Golda Meir.* New York: Chelsea House Publishers, 1985.

Sacher, Harry. *Israel: The Establishment of a State.* Westport, Connecticut: Hyperion Press, 1975.

Safran, Nadav. *Israel: The Embattled Ally.* Cambridge, Massachusetts: Harvard University Press, 1978.

St. John, Robert. *Ben-Gurion.* Garden City, New Jersey: Doubleday, 1971.

Chronology

Oct. 16, 1886	Born David Green in Plonsk, Poland
1897	Theodor Herzl founds the World Zionist Organization, a coalition of European Zionist groups, at a conference in Basel, Switzerland
1904–05	Green lives in Warsaw, Poland; works for *Poalei Zion,* a political party combining Zionism and socialism
Sept. 1906	Emigrates to Palestine, then a territory in the Ottoman Empire
1907	Joins an agricultural collective at Sejera, Galilee
1910	Moves to Jerusalem to work as an editor for *Achdut,* the Poalei Zion's newspaper; changes surname to Ben-Gurion
1915	Expelled from Palestine for conspiring to create a Jewish state
1915–18	Tours the United States speaking on Zionism
Nov. 2, 1917	Great Britain issues Balfour Declaration, expressing support for a Jewish homeland
Dec. 5, 1917	Ben-Gurion marries Paula Munweiss in New York City
1918	Serves in Egypt with a British battalion called the Jewish Legion
1920	Britain given a mandate to govern Palestine
1920–35	Ben-Gurion serves as general secretary of *Histadrut,* a federation of Jewish labor parties in Palestine
1935	Elected chairman of the Jewish Agency
1937	Britain's Peel Commission recommends partition of Palestine
1939	Britain issues White Paper, renouncing the Balfour Declaration and severely restricting Jewish immigration to Palestine
1939–45	Adolf Hitler's Nazi German government kills 6 million Jews
1945–46	Jewish armed resistance to British rule
1946	Ben-Gurion appointed defense minister in the Jewish Agency
1947	Britain gives up mandate; UN General Assembly votes for partition of Palestine
May 14, 1948	State of Israel established
1948–49	Israel fights War of Independence against five Arab nations
Jan. 1949	Ben-Gurion becomes prime minister after Israel's first elections
1952	Israel accepts reparations from West Germany
1953	Ben-Gurion resigns prime ministership and moves to Sdeh Boker, a kibbutz in the Negev
Feb. 1955	Returns to government as defense minister
Nov. 1955	Reappointed prime minister
1956	Israel, Great Britain, and France invade Egypt
June 15, 1963	Ben-Gurion resigns as prime minister
Dec. 1, 1973	Dies, aged 87, at Sdeh Boker

Index

Abdullah, king of Transjordan, 67, 69, 87
Achdut, 31
Achdut ha-Avodah, 40
Adenauer, Konrad, 88, 101
Alami, Musa, 49
Alexander II, tsar of Russia, 18
Algeria, 96
al-Husseini, Amin, 67
Allied Powers, 31, 35
Allon, Yigal, 72
Altalena, 72
Anderson, Robert, 96
anti-Semitism, 16–20
Aqaba, Gulf of, 87
Arab League, 61
Arab Legion, 65, 72
Attlee, Clement, 53, 56
Auschwitz, 52
Austria-Hungary, 31
Auto-Emancipation (Pinsker), 19
Balfour, Arthur, 37
Balfour Declaration, 37–39, 50
Bar-Zohar, Michael, 28
Basel, 21
Begin, Menachem, 52, 77, 88–89
Belorussia, 16
Ben-Gurion, Amos (son), 41
Ben-Gurion, David
    adopts new name, 31
    approves terrorist campaign against Britain, 56–57
    becomes newspaper writer, 31
    commands military, 63–67, 72–77
    death, 107
    early years, 16–23
    efforts as labor organizer, 23, 40–41
    emigrates to Palestine, 23, 25–26
    expelled from Palestine, 31–32
    final retirement, 106–107
    first retirement, 91–94
    foreign policy of, 87–89, 95–99, 101
    heads Jewish Agency, 45, 48–50, 52–53, 56–57
    proclaims independent state of Israel, 13–16
    significance of farming to, 26–29
    studies law, 31
    supports unlimited Jewish immigration to Israel, 83–84
    travels in United States, 32–35, 51–52
Ben-Gurion, Ge'ula (daughter), 35, 41
Ben-Gurion, Paula Munweiss (wife), 34–35, 41, 92, 107
Ben-Gurion, Renana (daughter), 41
Ben-Zvi, Yitzhak, 31–34
Bernadotte, Folke, 78–79
Bet-Halachmi, Yehezkel, 29
Bethlehem, 49
Bevin, Ernest, 56, 59, 65
Bible, 15–20, 27, 31, 92
Biltmore Conference, 52
Black Saturday, 57
Chagall, Marc, 14
Chamberlain, Neville, 50
Churchill, Winston, 53, 65
Circassian Arabs, 29–30
Commemoration (Ben-Zvi and Ben-Gurion) see *Yizker*
Constantinople, 31
Czechoslovakia, 50, 72
Daniel Deronda (Eliot), 18
Dayan, Moshe, 73, 93, 95, 102–103
Degania, 73
de Gaulle, Charles, 105
Deir Yassin, 68
Der Judenstaat (Herzl), 21
Dreyfus affair, 21
Dreyfus, Alfred, 21
Eban, Abba, 102
Egypt, 35, 66, 72, 77, 79, 81, 84, 93–99, 103–106
Eichmann, Adolf, 101–102
Eilat, 87, 91
Eisenhower, Dwight D., 95–98
Eliot, George, 18
Eretz Israel (Ben-Zvi and Ben-Gurion), 33
Eshkol, Levi, 105
Exodus, 59–61
Ezra, 21
France, 18, 37, 50–51, 72, 96–98
Galilee, 27–29, 73, 75, 77, 79
Gaza Strip, 79, 95, 97, 106
German Federal Republic see West Germany
Germany, 18, 21, 31, 47, 49–50
    see also West Germany
Gibly, Benjamin, 93–94
Golan Heights, 106
Great Britain, 18, 21, 35, 37–38, 44–45, 47–53, 55–59, 61, 63–65, 79, 87–88, 96–98

Green, Avigdor (father), 17, 19, 23, 26, 29
Green, David, *see* Ben-Gurion, David, early years
Green, Sheindel (mother), 17, 20
Green, Zvi Aryeh (grandfather), 17–19
Haganah, 39, 48, 52, 56–59, 63–66, 69, 71, 73, 75–76
Haifa, 58, 61
Hapoel Hatzair, 40
Hashomer, 31, 39
    see also Haganah
"Hatikvah", 15
Hebrew language, 15, 17–21, 27, 31, 39
Herzl, Theodor, 14, 21, 38
Hess, Moses, 18
Histadrut, 40–42, 103
Hitler, Adolf, 47, 49–53, 58
Holocaust, 52–53, 55, 88
Hovevei Zion (Lovers of Zion), 19
Hussein, sharif of Mecca, 37
Industrial Revolution, 16
Iran, 101
Iraq, 37, 84
Irgun, 52, 56–57, 65, 68, 77, 79
Italy, 37
Jaffa, 25, 48
Jerusalem, 28, 31, 44, 48–49, 57, 61, 66–67, 73, 75–77, 79, 81, 106
"Jew Holding the Tablets" (Chagall), 14
Jewish Agency, 39, 45, 48, 57, 63, 69
Jewish Legion, 35
The Jewish State (Herzl) *see Der Judenstaat*
Jordan, 87, 106
    see also Transjordan
Jordan River, 28, 106
Kalisher, Hirsch, 18
Kastel, 66
Katznelson, Berl, 42
Kenya, 21
King David Hotel, 57–58
Knesset, 86, 89, 94, 97–98, 101–103
Kollek, Teddy, 102
Kristallnacht, 47
Kurdistan, 28
Labor Zionists, 42, 45, 61
Labour party (Great Britain), 55–56
Latrum, 73–75
Lavon, Pinhas, 93–94, 103–104
Law of Return, 84
League of Nations, 39

Lebanon, 37, 81
Lehi, 52, 56, 68, 79
Lithuania, 16
London, 39, 53
Lovers of Zion *see Hovevei Zion*
Mabovitch, Goldie, *see* Meir, Golda
MacDonald, Ramsay, 45
Mapai, 40, 84, 86–87, 94, 102–104
Marshall, George, 69
Marx, Karl, 23
Mediterranean Sea, 28
Meir, Golda, 32, 69, 103–104
Milwaukee, 32
Montefiore, Moses, 18
Morocco, 84
Moyne, Lord, 52
Munich, 50
Munweiss, Paula, 34–35
    see also Ben-Gurion, Paula
Muslim Brotherhood, 87, 93
Nasser, Gamal Abdel, 93, 95–97, 99
National Council, 69, 71
Nazism, 43, 47, 49–53, 88
Negev desert, 79, 91, 93, 107
Nelkin, Rachel, 22–23, 25, 28–29, 34, 106
New York City, 32, 34–35
Nicholas II, tsar of Russia, 16
Nuremberg Laws, 47
Oliphant, Lawrence, 18
Operation Nachshon, 66–67
Osmon Pasha, Amin, 87
Ottoman Empire, 31, 35
Palestinians, 81
Palmach, 64, 72, 74
Paris, 47
Passfield, Lord (Sidney James Webb), 44
Peel Commission, 49
Peres, Shimon, 93, 102
Petach, Tikvah, 25–26, 92
Pinsker, Leon, 19
Plonsk, 17, 21, 23
Poalei Zion (Workers of Zion), 23, 31
pogroms, 17–18, 21
Poland, 16–17, 28, 51
Rafi, 104–105
Ramla, 65
Red Sea, 66, 87
Roosevelt, Franklin D., 55
Rothschild, Edmond de, 18, 26, 37
Rothschild, Lionel Walter, 37

111

Russia, 16–19, 28
Salvador, Joseph, 18
San Remo, 37
Sdeh Boker, 91–93, 106–107
Sejera, 27–29
Sharett, Moshe, 69, 93–95, 103
Sinai Peninsula, 79, 95–98, 105
Six-Day War, 106
Society of Friends of Learning, 17
Soviet Union, 61, 97
Sykes-Picot Agreement, 37
Suez Canal, 96, 105
Suez crisis, 96–99
Syria, 37, 65, 73, 81, 84, 106
Tel Aviv, 13–15, 48, 64, 71–73, 77
Tiran, Strait of, 95
Torah, 19
Transjordan, 37, 65, 67, 69, 72, 79, 81
   see also Jordan
Treblinka, 52
Truman, Harry, 55
Turkey, 25, 31, 101
Ukraine, 16
United Nations, 59, 61, 64–65, 69, 78–79, 98
United States, 32–35, 47, 52–53, 55, 61, 69, 79, 88, 95–96, 98
UNSCOP (United Nations Special Committee on Palestine), 59, 61
Wailing Wall, 44, 81
War of Independence, 65–69, 71–79, 81, 84, 91
Warsaw, 22
Webb, Sidney James, see Passfield, Lord
Weizmann, Chaim, 38–39, 45
West Bank, 106
West Germany, 88–89, 101
White Paper of 1930, 44–45
White Paper of 1939, 50–52, 55–56
Workers of Zion, see Poalei Zion
World War I, 31, 35, 39
World War II, 51–53
World Zionist Organization, 21, 38–39, 45, 49
Yadin, Yigael, 69
Yanait, Rachel, 31
Yemen, 28, 84
Yiddish, 18, 39
Yizker (Ben-Zvi and Ben-Gurion), 33
Yom Kippur War, 107
Yozhar, S., 81
Zemach, Shlomo, 22–23, 25
Zionism, 14, 18–23, 26, 28–29, 32–33, 37–39, 41–42, 45, 47, 50–53, 55, 61

John J. Vail is an Instructor in Political Science at Rutgers University, where he is currently a Ph.D. candidate. He received his B.A. from the University of Chicago. He has been a community activist in Chicago, San Francisco, and New York City. He is also the author of *Fidel Castro* in the Chelsea House series WORLD LEADERS PAST & PRESENT.

Arthur M. Schlesinger, jr., taught history at Harvard for many years and is currently Albert Schweitzer Professor of the Humanities at City University of New York. He is the author of numerous highly praised works in American history and has twice been awarded the Pulitzer Prize. He served in the White House as special assistant to Presidents Kennedy and Johnson.

165443